TEACHING THE BIBLE TO CHANGE LIVES

by

Kathy Hyde

HERE'S LIFE PUBLISHERS, INC.
San Bernardino, California 92402

TEACHING THE BIBLE TO CHANGE LIVES
by Kathy Hyde

Published by
HERE'S LIFE PUBLISHERS, INC.
P.O. Box 1576
San Bernardino, CA 92402

Library of Congress Catalogue Card 84-047801
ISBN 0-89840-064-3
HLP Product No. 950667
©1984, Kathy Hyde

All rights reserved.

Printed in the United States of America.

Unless otherwise indicated, Scripture quotations are from the New American Standard Bible, ©The Lockman Foundation 1960, 1962, 1963, 1968, 1971, 1972, 1973, 1975, and are used by permission.

Lovingly dedicated to the leaders of
Bible Discussion Groups who serve as
teachers, administrators,
group leaders and back-ups.

Contents

About This Book........................... viii
Foreword x

Section 1
A Handbook for Bible Discussion Groups

1. A New Experience..................... 1
2. Who, *Me* Lead a Bible Study?........... 11
3. Leading the Way...................... 17
4. Developing the Lesson................. 25
5. Directing the Discussion............... 43
6. Susan's Story......................... 67
7. Teaching the Wrap-Up................. 73
8. Starting the Class..................... 83
9. Training the Leaders.................. 91
10. Touching the World................... 97

Section 2
A Study in Colossians

Introduction 105

Lesson 1 Discussion Questions..............109
        Wrap-Up (Family Ties).............111

Lesson 2 Discussion Questions..............119
        Wrap-Up (Walking in Christ).......121

Lesson 3 Discussion Questions..............127
        Wrap-Up (Relating in Christ).......129

Conclusion—Pray, Plan, Persevere..........137

Appendix 141

About This Book

Have you ever wished you knew how to draw your non-Christian friends and neighbors into Bible study? Have you wanted a method whereby you could disciple Christians and send them out to win and teach others? This book outlines a Bible study method that is evangelistic in outreach and also facilitates "equipping the saints" for the ministry.

Section 1 is a handbook for leading Bible discussion groups.

Discussion groups are designed in three segments: home study, discussion, and teaching. Preparation for the class begins with the writing of Bible-centered discussion questions. One person or a small group develops intriguing questions for class participants to research at home.

Lessons studied at home are discussed in the first hour of class. Help for the leader of the discussion group is included in chapter 5. Simple, effective techniques are illustrated with conversations from actual group sessions.

Most classes, but not all, follow discussion with a 20-25 minute teaching session. Chapter 7 explains how to write and deliver a summary (wrap-up) of the Scripture lesson for the week. The wrap-up clarifies difficult points in the lesson and emphasizes application of the Scripture.

Section 2 ("A Study in Colossians") consists of sample lessons prepared especially for Bible discussion groups. Seven lessons are outlined, and three complete sets of questions and wrap-ups are printed. If you like, you may use the questions for a "trial class" to introduce the concept of a discussion group to your associates. The wrap-ups are included as ideas on how to tailor-make talks for the group you teach.

All illustrations are based on Paul's letter to the Colossians. The cast of discussion group participants introduced in chapter 1 appears throughout the book. In Ginny (new to Bible study) you may recognize your neighbor or friend. *You* may be Marilyn (the discussion group leader) or Susan (the teacher). The unnamed community in which the class meets could be *your* city.

Margins have been left wide for your use in making notes.

This book will give you the "how to's" for a Bible class. Let God give you the vision!

Foreword

When Kathy Hyde asked me to write the foreword to this book it brought back a collection of thoughts gathered through more than twenty years of observation. During those years, as has been the case with most pastors, I have concluded that Bible studies usually bring mixed blessings to the people of God. Yet the studies that have been developed according to the method described in this book have not been a mixed blessing—they have been *all* blessing.

Pick any observation point and the benefit becomes apparent. The studies have accomplished one thing few Bible studies achieve: They have brought spiritual support and stimulation to the churches represented by the study. While specific churches are never discussed, the people involved in the classes are encouraged continually to be contributing members within their own congregations. Beyond what the study does to develop the spiritual life of those who are in churches is the appeal to those who have no relationship with Christ.

From this pastor's point of view, the strongest feature of the approach presented is its ability to draw people who are outside of God's family into the study and bring them to a living relationship with the Savior.

The questions given for study and discussion, and the lecture delivered during the class, bring life on the fast track of this age and the Word of God together. Results include both evangelism and growth in Christian life.

How does all this happen? The best explanation is found in the basic principles espoused in what you are about to read. The approach presented is a method of studying the Bible so that it will change a person's way of living. It is not a collection of material about the Bible; it is a means of getting into the Bible. Each class is free to develop its own questions and each discussion group member is encouraged to discover and express what he or she has found through personal study. The Bible is allowed to be what God designed it to be—His Word for our lives.

Jim Rose

Pastor, Northwest Bible Church

Dallas, Texas

With Gratitude

Some time back my husband, Bob, bought me a new typewriter and laughingly said, "Now you can write a book. The words are in the typewriter; all you have to do is press the right keys!" At that time I had no intention of writing a book. I used the typewriter to prepare weekly lessons for Bible Discussion Groups and to write letters to leaders of classes that had formed in other cities, states and countries.

Realizing how many hours I spent answering letters, Bob again urged me to put it all down in book form. Finally, aware that God often gives me guidance through my mate, I started to write.

Friends encouraged me along the way. Becky Teter began calling me "Kathy Hemingway" and assured me that the book was needed and would be used by God to begin classes in hitherto unreached areas. Janet Boyden and Val Cox took on added responsibility for local classes to free my time for writing. Gene Ann Schwenk (my sister), Phyllis Ann Rose, and Mary Jones gave continual support and encouragement. Friends too numerous to mention by name prayed for the guidance of the Holy Spirit as I wrote.

Lyn Abercrombe, Nancy Hardin, Jena Brezinski, Johnnye Heaton and Lynna Lawrence read and critiqued the first few chapters. Their comments were invaluable. Margaret Hyde, Sue Edwards and Frank Brezinski took hours from their already packed schedules to help me over some rough spots. They will recognize their special contributions in the book.

Bible Discussion Groups board member and my pastor, Jim Rose, mailed five chapters to Les Stobbe at Here's Life Publishers. I am greatly indebted to Jim for setting the publishing process in motion. And I'm thankful to Les and his associate, Jean Bryant, for their guidance and skill in editing.

Last, but not least, I say thank you to my parents, Harry and Hazel Hyten, for their prayer support and example of Christian living. My mother's life verse for her children is taken from Psalm 112: 1, 2: "Blessed is the man that feareth the Lord, who delighteth greatly in his commandments. His seed shall be mighty upon the earth" (King James version).

Section 1
A Handbook for Bible Discussion Groups

1
A New Experience

"Well, I did it again," groaned Ginny as she flipped Frank's breakfast egg. "I agreed to go with Ann to her Bible study this morning. Can you see *me* in a Bible study?"

"Should be interesting!" Frank said as he grinned at her over the newspaper.

Ginny had agreed to go to please Ann, the neighbor she liked so well. Ginny and Frank and their two boys were new to the neighborhood, and the day they had moved in, Ann had brought over coffee and homemade cinnamon twists. The next day she had piled Ginny and the children into her station wagon for a brief tour of the city.

"Ann asked me that day she showed us around town," Ginny informed Frank. "She caught me off guard. I hope she's not one of those religious fanatics!"

"Keep Ann coming around! Maybe she'll bring us more of those rolls!"

I wonder what they do at those Bible classes, Ginny thought as she cleared away the dishes. *I'll go this once and then tell Ann it's just not my thing.*

Ginny had attended Sunday school as a child but found church boring. The few times she'd tried to read the Bible, it had seemed dull and confusing. The day Ann had talked about what she was learning from the book of Colossians, Ginny had listened politely, but without much real interest. Ginny didn't know if Colossians was in the Old Testament or the New Testament, but she didn't want to show her ignorance by asking. When Ann mentioned the writer of the book, the apostle Paul, Ginny started to comment, "Isn't he the one who was so down on women?" But out of consideration for her friend, she kept quiet. No matter how much she might disagree with Paul, she could spend one morning studying his writings for Ann's sake.

Ann pulled up in front of the house shortly after 9:00. She helped Ginny situate the diaper bags and buckle the children into the back seat.

Their first stop was the church nursery. The rooms were clean and cheerful, as was the nursery worker who met them at the door. "Any food allergies or special instructions?" she asked as she taped the boys' names on their belongings.

As the children began to play happily, Ann led the way into a large room where women were talking and laughing and drinking coffee. Ginny found herself caught up in a blur of friendly faces offering greetings like "Welcome to the class" and "We're glad you're here." She was just becoming acquainted with another recently transferred wife when she heard, "Last call for coffee! Let's get the groups started. It's almost 9:30!"

Ann whisked her off to a small room near the chapel, where she was given a name tag and a list of questions to be discussed during the coming hour. She sat down next to Ann in a circle shared by the ten or eleven women who attended the group regularly. As Ginny was presented to them, she saw a cross-section of the community: several young mothers, a newlywed, a grandmother, the wife of a seminary student, and an unmarried real estate agent who took Tuesday morning off to attend the class. As the morning progressed, Ginny learned that some of them, like herself, had never seriously studied the Bible, while others had much biblical knowledge. She found everyone in the group interesting, especially the group leader, Marilyn.

Marilyn skillfully drew Ginny into the conversation by asking about her children and her recent move. Ginny's negative attitude toward Bible study began to fade as Marilyn made it easy for her to relax and feel comfortable in the group.

Some of the things talked about during that hour gave Ginny a new concept of the Bible. It seemed much more up-to-date and practical than she had imagined. She especially liked the third question, which was drawn from Colossians 3:12-17. A woman named Barbara read these verses aloud, and Ginny thought they were lovely.

> And so, as those who have been chosen of God, holy and beloved, put on a heart of compassion, kindness, humility, gentleness and patience; bearing with one another, and forgiving each other, whoever has a complaint against any one; just as the Lord forgave you, so also should you. And beyond all these things put on love, which is the perfect bond of unity. And let the peace of Christ rule in your hearts, to which indeed you were called in one body; and be thankful. Let the world of Christ richly dwell within you, with all wisdom teaching and admonishing one another with psalms and hymns and spiritual songs, singing

with thankfulness in your hearts to God. And whatever you do in word or deed, do all in the name of the Lord Jesus, giving thanks through Him to God the Father.

Marilyn asked, "Using these verses as a guide, can someone pick out an action or an attribute she would like to develop to a greater degree in her own life?" The question intrigued Ginny.

Marge, the real estate agent spoke up. "I want to be more forgiving," she said with conviction, and then added that she had never been able to forgive her father for walking out on the family years before. She asked the women to pray for her, because her bitterness kept her from having a close relationship with her dad.

As Marge talked, another of the women, Kay seemed agitated and finally blurted out, "I think this is a bunch of pious nonsense! Why should we forgive people who hurt us? My parents were divorced, too, and I practically raised myself. Neither Mom nor Dad ever told me they were sorry their divorce messed up my life, and even if they did, I wouldn't forgive them!"

Shocked silence followed Kay's outburst. Marilyn, in her role as leader, moved quickly to ease everyone through the awkward moment. She spoke gently and reassuringly to Kay, telling her, "I don't think any of us realize the heartache you've felt. Forgiving others is a struggle for all of us."

Marge added, "I know exactly how you feel. It's tough growing up in a broken home."

These comments seemed to break the tension so the conversation could move on.

The most heated exchange took place on the subject of submission. Colossians 3:18 was read aloud: "Wives, be subject to your husbands, as is fitting in the Lord."

Then discussion began on what the Bible means when it instructs a wife to submit."

Barbara suggested that a wife should respect her husband's wishes. "If he asks her to spend less money or take his favorite shirt to the cleaners more often, she should do it happily."

Marilyn thanked Barbara for her input, then called on Ann. Ann proposed that a wife should back her husband in front of the children. Even if she didn't always agree, she should support him to show the children a united front.

"I object!" broke in Pat. "It's degrading to ask a woman to support a man when she knows he's wrong. She should tell her husband when he's out of line, showing the kids by her example that women do not give in to men just because they're men!"

Janet, the wife of a seminarian, jumped in quickly. "God has made the husband the head of the family, so it's important for his authority to be respected even if he happens to be wrong."

"I'm getting more and more confused," admitted Joy, the new bride. "I had never thought much about submission until I got married, and I can't seem to get a handle on it. Wasn't the Bible written for a less sophisticated culture and for women who considered men their superiors?"

Several participants broke in to answer Joy's question, but with all of them talking at once, she wasn't sure what was being said.

Marilyn laughingly interrupted. "Unless we take turns, Joy will never hear what we want to tell her! I think we all realize we are in a controversial area. There are many religious and cultural backgrounds represented in our group, so of course we will differ in our understanding of the Bible. Please feel free to state your opinions, but keep an open mind to other's ideas."

Ginny was impressed with Marilyn's handling of the situation and with her total acceptance of every viewpoint. She had always thought that Bible classes were designed to make everyone think one way (the "right" way), and it was refreshing to discover that controversial issues were considered from more than one viewpoint.

At this moment, Ginny decided that one week in the class wouldn't be enough. With such interesting exchanges taking place, she wanted to hear more.

Ginny sat quietly listening through the rest of the discussion on submission, but when the subject of prayer was introduced, she couldn't help interjecting, "Why do people pray, when God, if there is a God, already knows what He's going to do?"

Pat, speaking from her college background in psychology, responded, "I think praying makes us feel better. It's like going to a psychiatrist. When we can talk about our problems, they begin to look less terrifying."

"Are you saying that prayer is important only as an outlet for our emotions?" questioned Nancy, entering into the conversation for the first time. (She had not worked on her lesson before coming to class so hadn't felt prepared to contribute.)

"Basically, yes," answered Pat.

Nancy disagreed. "I'm sure praying does make us feel better, but I also think it puts us in touch with God. I've experienced so many answers to prayer that I think of it as much more than an emotional release."

Joy admitted that she had never seen an answer to prayer.

Marge suggested that praying made her feel less alone. "I talk to God about everything. I like to think He's a friend who cares what happens to me."

Janet added, "Prayer teaches me to depend on the Lord. I need His help in some way every day, and praying helps me maintain an attitude of dependence."

Marilyn thanked everyone for their stimulating comments. Ginny said, "I want to thank you, too. You've certainly given me food for thought."

Time passed quickly, and almost too soon the discussion hour was over. Marilyn dismissed the group, saying, "I'll look forward to seeing all of you again next week." She walked with Ann and Ginny toward the chapel and, on the way, explained to Ginny that at the close of the class, she would be handed a list of questions to be discussed the following week. She asked Ginny to read the chapter of the Bible from which the questions were drawn and jot down her comments on the study sheet. As they took seats in the chapel, Marilyn promised to telephone Ginny in a few days to give her additional help, if she needed it, in filling out her questions.

Ann had explained earlier that the class ended with a twenty-five minute message (wrap-up) by a

Bible teacher, which in Ginny's mind meant a dry talk by someone who wore outdated clothes and hadn't had a new idea in years. She was mistaken. The teacher, Susan Smith, turned out to be an attractive, articulate wife and mother who did not seem different from the other women in the class. Her approach to the Bible was practical and logical.

Much to Ginny's surprise, Susan did not draw on a special vocabulary. Ginny had heard words like "saved" and "sanctified" and doubted that she would ever be able to understand the Christian jargon. To her relief, Susan spoke in plain, everyday English. In an easy-to-understand way, she talked about the third chapter of Colossians, the same chapter covered in the discussion groups.

From Colossians 3:18—4:1, Susan traced a pattern for relationships involving husbands and wives, parents and children, employers and employees, Christians and non-Christians. She emphasized that families, friends and co-workers find their lives flowing together more smoothly when they follow biblical guidelines. She confessed that she herself sometimes failed to follow scriptural principles, and she drew from experience to illustrate that she, and those around her, were happier when her actions were based on God's Word. She challenged her audience to *apply* the teachings of Colossians 3 to everyday life and gave specific suggestions on how to do this.

Although Ginny didn't agree with everything she heard, Susan's clear presentation and willingness to discuss her own struggles was impressive.

As the wrap-up came to an end, Ginny's mind raced through the questions the Bible class had raised for her: *Can Scripture be taken as literally as Susan seems to think? Is God really interested in how I relate to my family and friends?*

After picking up the boys from the nursery, Ginny and Ann headed to Ann's house for lunch. Over sandwiches and coffee Ginny expressed her delight at the difference between her preconception of a Bible class and the actual encounter. She felt good about her experience with the group and was eager to return.

Wait till I tell Frank, she thought. *Won't he be surprised!*

2
Who, <u>Me</u> Lead a Bible Study?

Through Ginny's eyes you have just been introduced to a Bible study method that is growing in popularity among Christians, a Bible discussion group. Most groups are led by "non-professionals" —laymen, not theologians.

Women like Marilyn become deeply interested in God's Word. The Holy Spirit moves them to respond to the needs of friends and neighbors who do not know God personally. A Bible study results. One woman teaches a neighbor, or several Christians band together to form a larger class. The leaders of these groups prepare their own material, pray for and support one another, and give each other tips on leading discussion groups.

Ginny is typical of many women who join such studies and find that the Bible is more interesting and relevant than they ever suspected. It is both unexpected and intriguing to encounter a Bible class with a relaxed atmosphere in which questions can be asked without fear of sounding foolish and opinions can be stated without fear of rejection. Studying as they work on their question sheets, discussing the same passage of Scripture in the small group, and hearing the passage explained practically in a lecture have together constituted a life-changing experience for countless women.

The word of God changes lives, but how many discover that fact without a friend or acquaintance to introduce them to the study of Scripture? God uses Christians in the process of getting His Word into the hands (and hearts) of men and women like Frank and Ginny. *You* can be a part of the process. *You* can be the one to meet the Ginnys in your community and introduce them to Bible study. This is a "how-to" book. It's designed to present ideas and methods *you* can use to start a class in *your* neighborhood, *your* church, or *your* office. What is being done in other places can be adapted to your circumstances and your city.

My Own Experience

You may think that leading a Bible study is beyond your abilities. It isn't! If I could do it, so can you!

My experience in developing a Bible class began in 1966 in St. Petersburg, Florida. The class grew out of a chance encounter with a neighbor who told me she "used to be a Christian." She had at one time enjoyed going to church and taking part in church-oriented activities, but she had always had a great many questions about Christianity. On my suggestion, we began meeting one morning a week to look into the Bible for answers. I wrote out a few simple study questions to guide our search. The questions centered on what the Bible *says*, and how it *applies* to us. I did not know it then, but that two-person class would train me in the techniques necessary to work with a larger class.

Within a few months my neighbor moved to another state. Unless she reads this book, she will probably never know the far-reaching effects of the process she set in motion.

After she left Florida, other neighbors became interested in our Bible class, and the nucleus for a new group was formed. When it became apparent that several young mothers would join us if we provided baby-sitters, we moved from a home into a church with nursery facilities and pooled our money to hire workers.

As we moved into the church, I added a short teaching period to the class. The discussions usually ended with a few unresolved questions (which motivated us to study harder) and a vague sense of incompleteness. To tie up loose ends, I began delivering a summary (wrap-up) of the passages of Scripture covered that week.

Needs were being met, and the class continued to grow. Soon it was obvious that additional discussion leaders were needed. I could lead one group of fifteen, but what if the class grew to thirty or fifty?

The next major milestone was the beginning of a leaders' training course. Women who had been regular in attendance and exhibited enthusiasm and a desire to grow spiritually agreed to become leaders. We met together each week and by trial and error we developed guidelines for leading a discussion and teaching others to deliver wrap-ups.

Growth continued, and the process of division and planting began. Leaders moved away and started classes in new areas. Groups divided as they outgrew the home or church where they met. By 1974 there were several hundred women meeting throughout the Clearwater/St. Petersburg area. In 1975 my husband accepted employment in Dallas, Texas, and we left Florida. Because a number of leaders were trained and in place, the classes continued to flourish.

The last thing I expected to do in Texas was teach a Bible class. Dallas is in the middle of the Bible belt and probably has as many classes per capita as any city in the nation. I looked forward to sitting in an established study group where I could soak up the benefits of someone else's research and preparation. But my plans were not God's plans! The first neighbor I met told me she had always wanted to study the Bible but until recently had been too busy. Expectantly, I waited to see what would happen next!

My neighbor and I arranged to study together once a week. She was excited over our plans and invited several friends to join us. Six or eight women gathered in my living room that first Friday morning. In a few weeks the neighbor returned to her full-time job. She could no longer attend the class, but she had provided the initial impetus.

The pattern for the Florida classes was repeated in Texas as the process of growth, leadership training, and division began again. Soon there were groups throughout the Dallas area, and within two years classes had spread to distant places.

Something that began with two women, almost by accident, continues to expand and reach into new areas. Members now number several thousand

and the end is not yet in sight. New groups spring up almost weekly as more women catch the vision for reaching the world with God's Word.

Advantages of a Discussion Format

Why are Bible discussion groups successful? One key is the word "discuss." Many people are more open to *talking about* the Bible than they are to "being lectured at." The non-Christian and the new Christian especially appreciate the non-judgmental atmosphere in which they can speak freely without apprehension about how their comments may be received.

Individual Bible study is another key to success. Some group members spend only a few minutes a week preparing for the class. Others study for several hours. All come to class excited about the new and interesting truths they discover on their own. Those who have not fully answered their written questions learn from those who have. The ones who have studied diligently experience the satisfaction of sharing their greater knowledge. The interaction that takes place around God's Word stimulates everyone to appreciate and apply scriptural principles.

A discussion group also enhances fellowship. In the course of discussion, a participant can talk about her problems, triumphs and everyday experiences. Group members develop close relationships and begin to pray for and be concerned about one another.

Not every class adds a wrap-up after the discussion, but this segment is clearly advantageous as well. After hearing differing opinions in the discussion, group members appreciate a clear-cut exposition of Scripture. They are *ready* to hear God's

Word unfolded by a teacher who grasps the overall message of the Bible and can fit each section into a broader perspective. The wrap-up reinforces ideas learned in home study and discussion and explains how to *use* the knowledge gained. As each woman listens, she thinks, *This is meant especially for me.*

Results

Consider the impact of a Bible discussion group on someone like Ginny. Her life has been disrupted by a cross-country move and the loss of established friendships. She does not have a personal relationship with God to sustain her through her period of adjustment. Then she meets Ann (a new friend) and through Ann is introduced to a group of women she genuinely likes. She begins to study Scripture for herself and hears others in the class tell how God is working in their lives. This helps her to take the first steps toward trusting God herself. Before long Ginny may receive Christ as Savior and enter into eternal life.

This is a pattern that is repeated again and again in Bible discussion groups, but though it's familiar it never becomes less thrilling. It's a fresh, new miracle each time a class member finds Christ. Nor does the miracle end there. Each woman has family, friends, and neighbors who feel the effects of the class. When one life is changed, the ripples from that change touch countless lives.

The world is full of Ginnys waiting to be found. If you would like to be involved in reaching them with God's Word, read on. This book was written for you.

3
Leading the Way

Susan had in Marilyn qualities that would make her a good Bible discussion group leader. When she had approached Marilyn with the idea, Marilyn had been surprised because she had never considered herself a "leader." She had wondered, *Am I really the right person for the job? And would I be successful?*

What are the qualities God looks for in calling a person into a ministry? They are not the same aptitudes the business world looks for in an executive. The qualifications for a ministry are different from those sought by a secular employer.

A Leader Is a Christian

A Christian is personally related to God through Jesus Christ. A Christian believes that Christ died on the cross to pay her debt of sin (Rom. 5:8). A Christian has received Christ as Savior and is indwelt by the Holy Spirit (Rom. 8:11). To be a Christian is the first and most basic qualification for leadership in a Bible class.

A Leader Attends a Local Church

The Bible instructs Christians to assemble as a body for worship and instruction. A leader is obedient to God in faithful church attendance. She is loyal to her church, her pastor, and the believers with whom she worships.

A Leader Accepts the Authority of Scripture

A prerequisite for teaching the Bible is an acceptance of Scripture as God's truth for today. To believe it was written for another culture or an earlier age is to place it on a footing with any other literary work. The Bible is much more. It is God's timeless message to His people in all ages and all situations.

Can you accept Scripture as your standard day in and day out, even when it conflicts with the standards of society or your own personal choices? The Ginnys of the world watch to see if those who serve as Christian leaders actually live by the principles they espouse. Success in teaching the Word of God means living it out in practice.

A Leader Studies

A leader is an avid student of the Bible. As she studies, she asks the Holy Spirit to be her tutor; to point out truths she can apply to herself; to spotlight sins and habits that hinder her fellowship with God; to make the Scriptures come alive for her.

Last year's truth or even yesterday's truth isn't sufficient for today. Her desire to learn takes her back to Scripture every day.

A Leader Prays

Prayer is communication with God. As you study the Bible and pray, God speaks to you and you speak to Him. Prayer cannot be something you talk about but rarely work into your schedule; it must be a vital part of your life. In no other way can you know God as your friend, your teacher, your source of creativity, the one with whom you share a happy moment or an unsolved problem. As you open your heart to Him, you gain appreciation for who He is and for the powerful way He works to answer your prayers.

Who do you call when you have an urgent prayer need? It's the person you know will actually pray for you and keep praying until you receive an answer. A leader in a Bible class *is* that kind of person. She understands the importance of prayer for herself, for the other leaders in the class, and for the women who attend. God uses the class to change lives and glorify Himself as a leader prays.

A Leader Is Committed

To be a leader is to be in a position of sacred trust that cannot be entered into lightly. If you believe you are called to this ministry, you must be faithful to your calling. Your priorities must be in order. You must be able to say no to activities that would interfere with the time and energy needed to study and to be in contact with those you lead.

Almost certainly, once you commit to a Bible class ministry, other opportunities for service will present themselves. These may be worthwhile, even urgent needs. When you are tempted to add them to your already full schedule, however, ask yourself, *Will I become like my friend who always looks thrown-together and eats lunch while she dusts the living room?* Sometimes it is necessary to pass up good opportunities in order to concentrate on the best activities.

A Leader Is a Servant

In business, politics, or education, a leader is a person of stature—"the boss." He has authority and command. In contrast, the Bible defines a leader as a servant (Matt. 20:25-28). God's leader first serves Him, then as an outgrowth of that service, serves others.

In your position with a Bible class, you are simply a tool in God's hands, an instrument He can use to meet needs in the lives of the women with whom you work. Your example is Christ. Although He was God, He came to earth not to *be* served, but to serve (Mark 10:45).

A Leader Communicates Love and Affirmation

To effectively serve others, you must be genuinely concerned about them. You probably care deeply for people. Are you able to *show* you care? If your concern is not communicated, it's meaningless to anyone except yourself.

God's servant-leader looks for ways to convey love and warmth. She uses every opportunity to tell family members and friends, "I love you," "I enjoy being with you," "I care when you hurt," or whatever is appropriate to the occasion.

As the leader of a Bible class, you will need to relate quickly to new faces and to show concern for those you do not know well. You can increase your capacity to do this through practice. Wherever you go, initiate conversations and make those around you feel comfortable. In every situation (neighborhood gatherings, office parties, parent-teacher meetings, etc.), look for the person who seems lonely or alone. Talk to her. Draw her out with nonthreatening questions such as, "What brought you to our city?" or "Tell me about your children's school activities." Each time you set aside your own interests and concentrate on someone else, your ability to nurture and encourage will grow.

A Leader Is Open and Transparent

Members of a Bible class relate best to the leader who talks about her failures and shortcomings as well as her victories. Discussing her struggles with them endears her to them.

In a typical class will be women who are not yet Christians and Christians who have never grown past spiritual infancy. They desperately need to see someone who is working through frustrating habits and negative behavior patterns in response to God's guidance. Scripture abounds with men and women whose lives were transformed, but class members need to see a real-life transformation also—a leader who can say, "Yes, I'm struggling, but let me tell you what God is doing!"

In teaching the Bible class, Susan illustrates her wrap-ups with personal experiences. She doesn't hesitate to say, "I sometimes find it difficult to control my temper" or "Unless I'm careful, I get too demanding of my husband."

Marilyn, in leading her discussion group, admits to a tendency to worry and look at her circumstances rather than at God's provision.

Both Susan and Marilyn testify to God's faithfulness in helping them work through these problems. Their openness motivates class members to let God meet needs and work changes for them also.

A Leader Is a Good Listener

The following questions will help you rate yourself as a listener. It is hoped that you can answer yes to them all.

- Do you enjoy listening as much as you like talking?
- Do you encourage others to talk?
- Do you nod and smile and project an attitude of acceptance as you listen?
- Do you listen as attentively to a total stranger as you do to a friend or family member?
- Do you listen with an open mind even when you do not agree with what you hear?
- Do you listen "between the lines" for what is left unsaid (messages conveyed by tone of voice, facial expression, or gestures)?
- Do you pay complete attention to what someone is saying instead of mentally planning what you want to say in response?

Bible discussion groups draw women of all ages, from various social, economic, and religious backgrounds. Many are well-educated; a few are functionally illiterate. Some can express their thoughts easily, while others are very awkward in the art of verbal communication. No two women are exactly alike; therefore, each one has something unique to offer. Each one is worth listening to.

A Leader is Trustworthy

Many women begin attending a Bible class because they have emotional needs or are seeking help with problems. When you are in a position of leadership, they may confide in you, discussing with you difficult areas in their lives. You can *never*, under any circumstances, repeat anything not meant to be public knowledge.

A Leader Is on Time

A leader does not make a habit of keeping others waiting. She understands that running late destroys confidence in her ability to lead. Being in charge entails being *where* you say you'll be, *when* you say you'll be there.

Marilyn's discussion group members would feel unimportant if she rushed in late every week with excuses about last-minute phone calls or a stop to fill the gas tank. Even if her *intentions* were the best, consistently running behind schedule would undermine her relationship with the group and her effectiveness as a leader.

A Leader Is Well-Groomed

You say a lot by the way you look. Your manner of dress and general appearance convey how you feel about yourself and your role as a leader. Always make yourself as attractive as you can be.

Outer attractiveness results from careful attention to grooming. Inner beauty grows out of a vital relationship with God. Both are necessary in a leader.

YOU as a Leader

As you read the qualifications for leadership, did you find some of them different from what you anticipated? Contrary to what you might expect, it's not necessary that a leader have a great deal of biblical knowledge. More important is a desire to learn, a willingness to accept God's Word as authority, and a love for people.

Did you evaluate yourself against the qualities listed? Were you able to see your strengths and potential strengths? Stop a minute and thank God for them.

Did you pinpoint areas where change is needed? Accept their presence as a challenge to grow. Commit your weaknesses to God in prayer. Yield control of your life to Him, and ask Him to reshape you in those areas. By the grace of God, *become* the leader you know you can be.

Leaders Are Needed

There is always a shortage of true leaders. A leader is someone with whom others want to be. (By definition, she's a leader only if she has followers.) The Christian woman who possesses leadership qualities and skills attracts followers as a magnet attracts iron.

Many of your acquaintances do not have a vital relationship with their Creator. They lack guidelines to help them cope with the complex and confusing world in which they live. You may be the one God has chosen to lead them in a study of biblical principles. You can be His instrument to bring them into contact with a circle of honest, caring women who will reach out to them with love and acceptance. God may change lives because of your willingness to begin a Bible study group.

It is an exhilarating experience to watch God work as women study His Word. As a leader, it's a joy, a privilege and a reward to be involved in the process. All the hours of planning, praying and working become a labor of love.

The next chapter will tell you how to write discussion questions that will appeal to both Christians and non-Christians, novice studiers and those who have much knowledge. As you read, pray that God will give you new insight into Scripture and an excitement about preparing to teach women.

4
Developing The Lesson

This chapter is a guide to developing Bible-based questions for use with discussion groups. Questions can be written by the class teacher or by a *team* of leaders.

Knowledge of the Bible is the foundation for preparing lessons based on its teachings. Bible study is a life-long process. The greater the application to study, the greater the knowledge gained. It is not the purpose of this book to provide in-depth study methods, but the following suggestions will get you started.

1. Spend time each day reading the Bible. Establish a pattern that will get you into God's Word with regularity. Also carry a pocket-size Bible or a small New Testament with you wherever you go, and form the habit of reaching for it when you have a few uninvolved moments. As you read, visualize the situations described, and meditate on the meaning of each verse. Immerse yourself in God's Word, and gradually your understanding and love for it will grow.

2. Work through a good book on study methods. Josh McDowell's *Guide to Understanding*

Your Bible is very helpful.

3. Build a library of study aids. Invest in several different translations of the Bible. Add a good one-volume commentary, such as *The Wycliffe Bible Commentary*. Include a concordance for cross-referencing and a Bible dictionary for background information. Consult your local bookstore for suggestions on increasing your library further. Become familiar with the content of these books, and with how you can benefit from them.

4. Take notes each Sunday as your pastor preaches, and ask him questions about his sermons. Obtain his permission to telephone him if you have difficulty understanding the Scripture you are preparing for a Bible class.

In the process of absorbing Scripture, you will be preparing yourself to teach others. How do you learn? Bit by bit. How do others learn? The same way. Therefore, one of your first tasks will be to break Bible study into bite-size pieces that can be easily assimilated. You can do this over a period of weeks or months before actually beginning the class.

Writing Questions

Informal discussion can be fun but is not necessarily productive. For that reason, written questions are prescribed for Bible discussion groups. The development of the questions is key to the success of the discussion, so a detailed methodology is provided to guide you in formulating lesson material.

Discussion group leaders outline passages of Scripture paragraph-by-paragraph and subject-by-subject. This material is then shaped into question-and-answer form. The questions provide a study guide for class members and invite their active participation in the class. To illustrate how questions are developed, Colossians 3:1—4:6 will be used as a model. Keep in mind, however, that this method can be applied to any part of the Bible.

To begin writing questions, choose a section of Scripture with which to work. Select a portion you particularly *enjoy* studying. If you have a special liking for the material, you will communicate enthusiasm as you write. The section you choose may be an entire book or part of a book, such as a selection of Psalms or Proverbs. Read the section several times in different translations of the Bible to increase your grasp of the passage.

Step One—Summary of Paragraph   (see page 28)

Sit down with a *paragraphed* Bible and a three-column chart in front of you. Title the first column "Summary of Paragraph." In this column, jot down *in your own words* a brief synopsis of each paragraph. Stick to the facts—what is actually said or clearly implied. If you are confused about what the facts *mean*, do some research with a commentary or concordance, and add the information to your notes in column one. But do your own study first. You will be amazed at how enjoyable it is to discover truth for yourself. Depend on commentaries only for background material, biographical sketches, and other information you would not be able to find in the text itself.

Summary of Paragraph	Personal Application	Discussion
Col 3:5-11 Christ is to be the focus of the thoughts & actions of the Christian (3:1-4). No negative traits should be eliminated from Christian character. Paul lists sexual sins, greed, anger, lying etc. as part of the old life without Christ	Paul points out sins & habits that have no place in my life. The Holy Spirit is working to produce Christ character traits in me (Rom 29). If no work is done in this in the Spring again	Does Col Paul is that is Christ about anger to to attend all is it

Summary of Paragraph	Personal Application	Discussion Questions
Col 3:5-11 Christ is to be the focus of the thoughts & actions of the Christian (3:1-4). The negative traits should be eliminated from the Christian. Paul instead of dying as part of the old that...	Paul points out sins & habits that have no place in my life. The Holy Spirit is working to produce Christ's character traits in me (Rom. 8:29). I must work with him in this process so he won't change me against my will.	In Col. 3:1-3 Paul indicates that what Christians think about is important. How do terms like attention to attitudes & actions. Get down the negative & ills. I the good. How is their li- attitude

Summary of Paragraph	Personal Application	Discussion Questions
Christ is the focus of thoughts & aim of the Christian (3:1-4)	Paul points out sins + habits that have no place in my life. The Holy Spirit is working to produce Christlike character traits in me (Rom. 8:...). I must walk with Him + prove work + will	In Col. 3:1-3 Paul indicates that what Christians think about is important. How is this tied to attitudes & actions. List down the negative qualities believers must get out of their lives entirely. (vv. 5-9)

3:5-11

Step Two—Application   *(see page 29)*

"Personal Application" is a good heading for column two of your chart. Here you take the facts and relate them to life. As you write, ask yourself, *Is there a lesson in this for* me? and *How can I use it in my life today?* Once you understand how a passage applies to you, you will know how to help others apply it to themselves.

Step Three—Questions   *(see page 30)*

Column three will flow logically out of the first two columns. Call it "Discussion Questions." After you know the facts of Scripture and how they apply, it is not difficult to structure the information into question form.

My entire chart for Colossians 3:1—4:6 is included at the end of this chapter. However, if *you* chart these chapters, your finished product will be influenced by your unique background, experience and mental grid. Your perspective on this passage will be different. In preparing study material, it is important that you do your best to convey the meaning of Scripture accurately (don't take liberties), but expect your work to reflect your individual personality and way of thinking.

As you write, strive to make Scripture understandable and applicable. Emphasize main themes rather than concentrating on a few verses. Add interest by using variety in style and wording. Become familiar with different *types* of questions, and incorporate as many as possible into each lesson.

1. *Background Question.* As a general rule, ask for background information in the first lesson of a new series. This ties the Bible into history and sets the scene for the book you are studying.

Examples: Describe the city of Colossae using information you find in an encyclopedia or Bible dictionary.

What problems were the Colossian Christians experiencing? (If you have access to background material, do some research on this question.)

2. *Factual Question.* This question can be answered directly from Scripture.

Examples: In writing to the Colossians, how does Paul describe himself? How does he describe them? (Col. 1:1,2)

Colossians chapter 1 tells us that knowledge is not meant to be an end in itself. According to verse 10, knowledge should lead to....

Every lesson should contain some questions that can be answered by the least experienced participant in the class. A simple factual question will enable even those who are brand new to Bible study to contribute to the discussion.

This type of question can also be used to drive home a point. Writing out the facts emphasizes them and causes them to be remembered.

3. *Challenge Question.* A challenge question is designed to make studiers stretch their minds and search the Scriptures for answers that are not immediately obvious. Not everyone will be able to answer these questions, but those who cannot will learn from those who can.

Examples: Try to form a clear idea of what it means to be buried with Christ in baptism and raised to new life in Him (Col. 2:11). Explain this in very simple terms.

Challenge question for those who like to do research: Explain Colossians 2:15.

4. *Personal Experience Question.* Everyone is an expert on her own experience. Give every class member an opportunity to participate in the discussion by asking personal experience questions. Even the least knowledgeable woman can respond with confidence to a query concerning herself. As she talks about the events of her life, others come to know her and begin to love her.

Examples: Tell us about an experience that taught you the importance of drawing on God's strength in a difficult situation.

Have you ever reached out by letter, as Paul did, to give someone support and encouragement? What did your thoughtfulness mean to him/her?

5. *Personal Opinion Question.* An opinion is a personal judgment. "I think" or "My opinion is" may not always line up with the facts, but it still needs to be said. Everyone likes to feel that her opinions count.

Examples: Why to you think God allows Christians to experience suffering and hardship?

In your opinion, why does God instruct a wife to submit to her husband?

Few people like being *told* what to think; they would rather arrive at their own conclusions. Encouraging a woman to express her opinions clears the way for further learning and the acceptance of ideas she may previously have rejected.

A personal opinion question is useful in another way, too. When a leader hears "I think" from a class member, it gives her a valuable clue to the woman's value system and spiritual development.

6. *Application Question.* To learn biblical facts is of little worth unless those facts are applied. An application question asks, "How does this passage apply to me?" "Have I been applying it?" "How can I start applying it?"

>Examples: "Christ in you, the hope of glory" is a key concept in the book of Colossians. What difference does Christ in *you* make in your daily living? (Or, if you are not yet a Christian, what difference do you think it *might* make?)
>
>Paul desired that all Christians be "knit together in love" (Col. 2:2). If you know how to knit, describe the process (or bring knitting needles and give a demonstration). Give your ideas on how the principle of being knitted in love can be applied in this class.

7. *Therapy Question.* Although it is part of the application process, a therapy question engages the mind and emotions on a deeper level. It causes self-examination and re-evaluation. It exposes problems and prejudices to the light of God's Word. It provides opportunity for change and growth.

>Examples: The Bible teaches forgiveness. Is it hard for you to forgive those who hurt you? How can you become a more forgiving person?

Being honest with yourself, make note of what you spend the most time thinking about. Is this the subject that *should* occupy the center of your thoughts? Why or why not? (Consider Col. 3:1—3 and Phil. 4:8)

Writing various types of questions will prevent class conversation from becoming dull. Variety is important, too, when apportioning time in the discussion hour. A simple factual question takes very little discussion and can be passed over quickly; personal views or application questions need more time. Too many factual questions and the group will finish too soon. Too many more-involved questions and the lesson cannot be completed in an hour.

Questions should be as open-ended as possible. Both Christians and non-Christians should be able to answer most of them without feeling cornered. The truth of Scripture should not be compromised, but there should be leeway for a number of different answers.

Formulating questions will teach you more of God's Word and give you confidence in handling the discussion generated by the questions.

Assignment

Now it is time for you to write your own set of questions. This exercise is the first step in developing *your* skill at composing questions.

The charts for Colossians 3:1—4:6 are attached to this chapter. Make your own chart of Colossians chapter 1 or 2. Use columns titled "Summary of Paragraph," "Personal Application," and "Discussion Questions."

After writing your questions, compare your work with the questions in the Colossians study in section 2. You will notice both differences and similarities. Check to see if you achieved a balance between the seven types of discussion questions:

BACKGROUND
FACTUAL
CHALLENGE
EXPERIENCE
OPINION
APPLICATION
THERAPY

SUMMARY OF PARAGRAPH	PERSONAL APPLICATION	DISCUSSION QUESTIONS
Col. 3:1-4 The Christian has "died" (died to his old way of life dominated by sin) and been raised to new life in Christ (eternal life, resurrection life). Therefore the thoughts of Christ's people should focus on Him and the life they have in Him, rather than on matters that keep them earth-centered. Christ is now seated at the right hand of God. At some future time He will be seen by everyone and Christians will be seen with Him.	What I think about is important. I need to form the habit of thinking about Christ (who He is, what He has done for me, how He sees my circumstances, and the life I will have with Him in the future). Christ will never have His rightful place in my thoughts unless I consciously place Him there. I will never see my circumstances from the proper perspective unless I adopt His perspective.	Col. 3:2 in the New American Standard Bible is translated "Set your mind on the things above, not on the things that are on earth." Paraphrase this verse in your own words, relating it to yourself and your thoughts. Being honest with yourself, make note of what you spend the most time thinking about. Is this the subject(s) that should occupy the center of your thoughts? Why or why not? Consider Col. 3:1-3 and Phil. 4:8.
3:5-11 Christ is to be the focus of the thoughts and actions of the Christian (3:1-4), so negative traits should be eliminated from Christian character. 3:5-9 list sexual sins, greed (which Paul equates with idolatry), anger, lying, etc. Such sins are part of the old nature and the old life without God.	Paul points out sins and habits that have no place in my life as a Christian. The Holy Spirit is working in me to produce Christ's character traits (Rom. 8:29). I must work *with* Him in this process and stop doing things I know will displease Him. He will not change me against my will.	In Col. 3:1-3 Paul indicates that what Christians think about is important. Then he turns his attention to attitudes and actions. Jot down the negative qualities he tells believers to put out of their lives entirely (vv. 5-9). How do you think someone can go about eliminating these negatives? Be

SUMMARY OF PARAGRAPH	PERSONAL APPLICATION	DISCUSSION QUESTIONS
Christians are being renewed and changed into the likeness of Christ. In this renewing there is no distinction between Jew and Greek, circumcised and uncircumcised, slave and free.	God is equally at work in *all* His people. Cultural background or social position or any other "difference" does not matter.	

3:12-17

God's people are to practice positive actions and attributes such as compassion, humility, gentleness, patience, forgiveness, love, peace, thankfulness, etc. The admonition is given to study and live by God's Word, to teach and to admonish (warn or correct) by means of "psalms and hymns and spiritual songs." All is to be done in the name of Christ, with thanksgiving.	Verses 5-17 constitute a test whereby I can determine at any moment if I'm living by the power and control of the Holy Spirit or if I'm self-centered and sin-centered. The negative characteristics listed in verses 5-9 must be replaced with positive attributes (vv. 12-17). A vacuum is quickly filled with *something*, so displacing the negatives is not enough — positives must be added. To aid me in developing the right at-	List the desirable qualities mentioned in 3:12-17. From the above list, choose one attitude or action you would like to develop to a greater degree. Explain *why* you chose this particular attribute. How do you plan to develop it?

SUMMARY OF PARAGRAPH	PERSONAL APPLICATION	DISCUSSION QUESTIONS
	titudes and behavior patterns, I need to be studying the Bible myself, plus joining with other believers in study and worship of God.	
3:18-21 *Family Relationships* 3:18 Wives: submit to your husbands. SUBMIT: to yield voluntarily.	God has chosen to make my husband the leader in our home. Part of my obedience to God is to willingly and voluntarily accept my husband's leadership.	In Col. 3:18 Paul instructs wives to "submit" or to "be subject" to their husbands. Define submission as it is used in the Bible. See Eph. 5:21-24. Describe to the group your *feelings* about submission. Does being submissive mean a wife never express an opinion or disagrees with her husband? Explain your answer. It takes strength and courage for one person to willingly submit to another. Christ demonstrated these qualities when He submitted to His Father. (Phil. 2:5-8). How can you gain more of His kind of strength and confidence?

SUMMARY OF PARAGRAPH	PERSONAL APPLICATION	DISCUSSION QUESTIONS
3:19 Husbands: love your wives; don't be harsh with them. LOVE: To seek the best for the other person no matter what the cost. God so *loved* that He *gave* His own Son (John 3:16).	God tells me to submit to my husband and instructs him to love me. As we both obey God, our relationship is harmonious and strong.	Submission on the part of a wife is basic to God's plan for a beautiful marriage. Equally vital to the health and happiness of this relationship is the responsibility God gives the husband to love his wife (3:19). Define the word "love" as it is used in Scripture. See John 3:16, 1 John 3:16, John 15:12, 13, Eph. 5:25. Tell your group about something special your husband has done to show his love for you.
3:20, 21 Children: Obey parents. Fathers: (probably refers to both parents) don't exasperate or irritate your children.	God instructs children to obey their parents, but since obedience does not come naturally, this is something I must teach my child. To achieve the best results, obedience must be balanced with sensitivity.	In verses 20, 21 the emphasis shifts from husbands and wives to parents and children. Discuss the factors that bring balance and harmony into this relationship.

SUMMARY OF PARAGRAPH	PERSONAL APPLICATION	DISCUSSION QUESTIONS
3:22—4:1 Slaves: Obey masters, do everything cheerfully and enthusiastically, for Christ's sake, knowing the reward will come from Him. The man who wrongs another will receive the consequences of his act (Implied: God will see to it). Masters: Be fair and just in dealing with slaves, knowing you have a Master in heaven.	I am to treat anyone I employ generously and fairly. When I am employed by another person, I am to work hard and enthusiastically. (I serve God by serving well the one who hires me. God will reward me for good service.)	What does Paul say about the master-slave relationship in 3:22—4:1? State the principles found in this passage that can be carried over into today's society.
4:2-4 Prayer is to be consistent and persevering, with thanksgiving. Paul asked believers to pray for him as he was in prison; asked specifically for open doors (opportunities to preach the gospel).	Family, friends and acquaintances *depend* on me to pray for them, so I need to make prayer on their behalf an everyday priority. Prayer helps to meet their needs *and* strengthens the bonds between us, because by praying I am having a part in their lives. God moves to meet *my* needs and change *my* circumstances as they pray for me.	What general instructions on prayer are given in 4:2? Paul illustrates the importance of prayer and the importance of Christian relationships as he asks the Colossians to pray for him. He expected their prayers to open doors of opportunity for the spreading of the gospel (4:3, 4). Just as Paul depended on others to pray for

SUMMARY OF PARAGRAPH	PERSONAL APPLICATION	DISCUSSION QUESTIONS
	My prayers should include thanksgiving as well as petition, and I should expect to see answers (open doors).	him, so someone depends on your prayers. Who do you pray for on a consistent basis? (Or who would you like to begin praying for?) What doors do you expect to see open for them as you pray?
4:5, 6 Paul adds to his guidelines for relationships by telling Christians how to conduct themselves toward those on "the outside" (non-Christians). Wisdom, gracious words and perceptive answers are to be the governing factors. This turns each contact with an unbeliever into a witness for Christ (uses time to best advantage).	I am a representative of Christ to the non-Christian world. My conduct and my words will either be a good witness or a poor one. If I live as instructed in Col. 3 and 4, I will be the kind of representative I should be.	According to 4:5, 6, how are Christians to relate to those who are not Christians?
4:7-18 Miscellaneous greetings and salutations.		

5

Directing the Discussion

Think back to the last time you took part in a really stimulating discussion. Perhaps your pulse quickened as your minds raced to put your thoughts in order. You verbalized your ideas clearly and responded enthusiastically to the conversational give and take. Exhilarated, you wished every discussion could be as satisfying.

What occurred spontaneously on that occasion can happen more often when you understand some of the factors that make the difference between an engrossing conversation and a dull one. For instance. (1) the subject is one of those factors. It's easy to be stimulated when you talk about something you find intensely interesting. (2) The manner in which the group interacts is important. A good flow of conversation gives everyone a chance to participate. No one person dominates. (3) A true "discussion" allows for differences of opinion. Ideas can be exchanged without anyone's feeling threatened. (4) There is openness and honesty. It's all right to say, "I have a problem. Can someone tell me what to do?" (5) There is room for reevaluation and change. A participant can admit, "I guess I was wrong. I hadn't thought things through as well as I should have."

Chapter 1 introduced you to a group leader named Marilyn who applied the principles of good discussion to a Bible class. Marilyn was not a teacher of the Bible, but rather a facilitator of stimulating conversation centered on biblical topics. She didn't instruct, answer questions, or correct "wrong" answers. She drew information and ideas from class members and fostered a relaxed atmosphere that made conversation easy. The women in her group thought her words came naturally and without effort. Only Marilyn knew that everything she said and did resulted from training and preparation. When she became a Bible class leader, she was taught how to guide discussion into productive channels.

The remainder of this chapter will tell *you* how to lead a discussion group as skillfully as Marilyn. The setting will be a Bible class, but the basic principles for guiding discussions can be applied in any arena. When a family gathers around the dinner table, the environment is ripe for talking and exchanging news of the day's events. When friends meet in the supermarket or at a neighborhood party, the scene is set for discussion. Good conversation can take place in an airport, in an office building, or over the back fence.

Setting the Stage

Plan the setting for your Bible discussion group. Whether you meet in a home, church, or elsewhere, consider comfort and visibility. Check for adequate lighting. Arrange chairs in a circle (or as near a circle as possible in your surroundings) so each person can be seen by all the others.

Since it is often difficult to remember names, make it easier by providing name tags.

If convenient, serve coffee or iced tea to help promote an informal, relaxed atmosphere.

Set the tone for the meeting by greeting with warmth and enthusiasm each woman who attends. Picture yourself as hostess to the most important women in the world at the gathering you have looked forward to all week. (Think, *I'm glad I'm here; I'm glad she's here!*) By attitude, words and gestures, convey to each one how much you like being with her. Smile. Laugh. Reach out and touch.

Naturally, this warmth ought to be genuine. Your call to a ministry of leading a Bible study must be motivated by a deep concern for the women you will teach (1 Cor. 13). Besides, if you do not have this motivation and try to fake a display of concern, the women in your group will soon see through it.

As you circulate, remember that not everyone knows how to initiate friendships. Introduce visitors, and see that each women has a conversational partner.

As mentioned in chapter 3, a leader is known for her ability to stick to a time schedule. Nowhere is this more important than in conducting a Bible class. Start the discussion *promptly* at the hour announced. Urge class members to arrive early to talk with each other, but keep an eye on the clock to see that the socializing does not run into the class time. Don't hesitate to break into the chit-chat! On this occasion, being too polite to interrupt will work against you. Women on tight schedules will count on you to start on time and finish on time. Others will habitually arrive late and out of breath. Don't wait for them! They will try harder to be punctual if running late means they miss some of the discussion.

Beginning the Discussion

A good beginning to the discussion hour is important. Again your attitude and the enthusiasm with which you speak will greatly influence the mood of the group.

One way to launch the discussion is to give a short recap of the previous lesson, tying it into the current lesson. This provides a review for those who attended the week before and brings those who were not present up-to-date.

You may want to begin the hour with a short prayer. Lead the prayer yourself rather than asking someone else. In this way you protect group members from possible embarrassment. Many women have never prayed aloud and may not return to class if they think you might ask them to do so.

Occasionally, spend five or ten minutes at the start of the class on a get-acquainted question. The better the women know each other, the closer they will feel. "Tell us something about yourself we wouldn't be able to guess by looking at you" usually provokes an absorbing array of answers. So does, "If you had a week with an eighth day in it, what would you do with the extra day?" Be creative in devising questions, and center them on the woman herself, not on her family. Hearing she has three children isn't nearly as fascinating as learning she writes poetry or works part-time as a plumber's helper.

From the first moment with your group, display a manner of authority (subtle rather than overpowering) and a firm hand in directing the discussion process. You are the one in charge, so act the part. Use your training and ability to keep the conversation on track. Be firm, be gentle; in control, but not bossy.

>SETTING: The discussion group.
>
>QUESTION: *Have you ever reached out by letter, as Paul did, to give someone support or encouragement? What did your thoughtfulness mean to him/her?*
>
>Marilyn: "Who would like to start us off on this question?"
>
>Pat: "I hate to write letters, so I use the telephone instead. However, I have a problem. I can't always cut off the conversation when I want to. Some of my friends could talk for hours! How do the rest of you handle long phone calls?"
>
>Kay: "One thing that seems to work is—"
>
>Marilyn: "Excuse me, girls. I really do understand your problem, but the subject of using the telephone to the best advantage could lead us into a long discussion. Since our time is short, let's cover the printed questions first; then if we have time at the end of the hour we can talk about telephoning. I'm sure it would be of interest.
>
>"Now, would someone who answered yes to question one please relate her experience in writing letters?"

Encouraging Interaction

What can a leader do to promote a lively discussion? Several things. After reading the question aloud, she can *call on* a few participants for their ideas. They will be prepared to answer because they have studied a designated section of Scripture before coming to class and have in hand a copy of the questions to be discussed. Calling on a few outgoing women who enjoy talking moves things along.

Once conversation begins to flow, the leader can let volunteers carry the conversation forward. She doesn't need to interrupt unless she observes that a few women are dominating, while others who would like to talk are being overlooked.

SETTING: The discussion group.

QUESTION: *Colossians 2:6, 7 instructs those who know Christ as Savior to "walk in Him" or "live in Him." How is this done?*

Marilyn: "Janet, I'd like to hear what you have to say! This is the type of question you always seem to enjoy."

Janet: "You're right! I love the questions I can get my teeth into. I have almost two pages of notes, but I'll try to summarize.

"According to my Bible dictionary, the word 'walk' refers to all our activities. Therefore, for me to walk in Christ means that I consider Him in everything I do from the moment I get up in the morning until I go to bed at night. To be able to do this, I must be rooted in Christ and built up in Him, as verse 7 indicates.

"To be rooted is just what it sounds like. When a tree takes root, it becomes firmly attached to the soil from which it takes its nourishment. When a Christian takes root, he becomes strong in faith. To 'build up' means to build *upon* something. As I understand it, the foundation for the building process is a person's salvation experience. First a foundation is established, then a building process can begin."

Marilyn: "I really appreciate the time and effort you put into your questions. Thank you for sharing your research with us and allowing all of us to benefit from it.

"Barbara, how did you answer this question?"

Barbara: "I'm sorry; I didn't have time to do the questions this week."

Marilyn: "I'm glad you came to class anyway Barbara. Ann, can you add to the discussion?"

Ann: "I think of walking as putting one foot in front of another and then repeating the process, trusting Christ in each step. The first step was trusting Him to be my Savior. The following steps take me along the road to spiritual maturity. The more I practice putting one foot in front of the other, the more progress I make."

Marilyn: "That's a beautiful illustration we will all remember. I'm glad I called on you.

"Let's hear one more answer. How about a volunteer?"

Joy: "I personalized this question. I've been having a terrible time getting along with my mother-in-law, and when I read about 'walking in Christ,' I decided that every time I had contact with her I would ask myself, 'If Christ were walking in my shoes, what would He do? I can't tell you the difference it's made! She and I are starting to have the relationship I've always wanted but didn't know how to achieve."

Marge: "Joy, you've just given me an idea! I have a neighbor who drives me up the wall! I wonder what would happen if I did with her what you've done with your mother-in-law?"

Ginny: "The idea of walking in Christ intrigues me, but I don't think it's realistic. If I'm always thinking, *What would Christ do?*, I'll end up playing a role and trying to be someone I'm not. It will all be phony!"

Janet: "It's not phony if you've first taken the step of accepting Christ as Savior. Then you have His Spirit living in you, and He gives you both the desire and the power to act as He wants you to act."

Nancy: "I have a book at home that helped me to understand the changes that take place in us when we become Christians. I'll loan it to you, Ginny, if you want to read it."

Ginny: "Thank you, I would."

Kay: "I'd like to read it, too."

Marilyn: "I've learned a lot hearing this question answered so many different ways. My thanks to all of you for your suggestions.

"Since we've pretty well covered this subject, shall we move on to the next question?"

Notice that Marilyn set the discussion in motion by calling on Janet and Ann. Then volunteers took over. Joy's comments sparked Marge to see a practical application for her own life. This led Ginny to confess her doubt that she could "walk in Christ" herself. Janet and Nancy stepped in to help Ginny and discovered that Kay, too, was looking for answers. Marilyn stayed out of the picture as long as the conversation moved in an interesting, profitable way. When she saw it winding down, she again took charge.

A good general rule to remember when you lead a group is to call on group members by name (1) at the beginning of the hour, (2) when you introduce a new subject, or (3) when you feel the need to quicken the pace of the conversation. Allowing volunteers to speak spontaneously will make for a more natural conversational pattern. However, do not depend on volunteers if the conversation wanders away from the main topic or if one person dominates the discussion. Call on someone.

Personal Questions

It's *never* appropriate to call on a woman to answer a question that might cause her to reveal something intensely personal. It's all right to ask a class member, "After studying chapter 2 of Colossians, do you think it's possible for the average person to become more forgiving?" *Under no circumstances*, however, should a leader ask, "Who do you find it difficult to forgive?" or "Do you harbor grudges after telling someone he or she is forgiven?"

Leave the personal questions strictly to volunteers. A few women are always willing to talk about their own problems and shortcomings. (This is an area where you as a discussion leader can be open, too. Leaders are instructed not to answer questions, but can feel free to talk about personal experiences.) One of the great benefits of a discussion group is the therapy that takes place when participants begin to open up about their struggles, fears, or feelings of inadequacy. The leader (or another volunteer) can set this process in motion by being honest and open about herself. As others in the group hear her story, they will add theirs, often commenting, "I thought I was the only one with that problem." What has been an individual concern then becomes a shared experience that draws the women closer to each other.

The "Right" Answer

What does a discussion leader do when a group member asks her for the "right" answer to a question? She explains that in a discussion it's not necessary for everyone to think the same way or arrive at the same conclusions. Answers are not labeled "right" and "wrong." When asked for answers, state that your function is simply to guide the conversation, not to see that the group agrees on one "correct" answer.

SETTING: The discussion group.

QUESTION: *Explain Colossians 2:15: "When He had disarmed the rulers and authorities, He made a public display of them, having triumphed over them through Him."*

Janet: "As I researched this verse I came to the conclusion that—"

Joy: "This verse was totally confusing. I didn't even try to explain it."

Nancy: "I asked my pastor what it meant, and he told me—"

Marge: "I got very frustrated trying to answer this question. I must have spent an hour looking up cross-references and trying to understand it, but I just couldn't. Hearing what Janet and Nancy said doesn't help much either. Marilyn, you're our leader, will you please tell us what this verse is supposed to mean?"

Marilyn: "To be honest, I struggled with this question myself, and I intend to do more reading and studying this week. Rather than my telling you what I think, I'd like to suggest that we all do a little further study and talk about this again at a later date—maybe when we get together for lunch next Tuesday.

"Marge, if you feel you need a more satisfactory answer today, you might speak to our teacher, Susan Smith, after the wrap-up. She's spent several months preparing to teach Colossians, and I'm sure she will gladly give you any information she has.

"If no one else want to talk about this question, let's go on to the next one. It's really not necessary that we answer every question completely. The purpose of a discussion is to exchange ideas. We don't have to come up with hard and fast answers.

Separating the role of the discussion leader from that of a teacher frees the women from fear that the leader wants to check their work or judge their comments. An added benefit is that she does not need an in-depth knowledge of Scripture. Even if relatively new to Bible study, she can function as a group leader. She is being trained by the class teacher and works under the teacher's authority. The teacher is the one the class looks to for an overall knowledge of the Bible. In a typical class, a number of discussion leaders never teach, but they do learn biblical basics week by week along with their group. (The discussion leader who is also a teacher must be careful not to turn the discussion hour into a teaching session. The discussion setting is for class participants to share *their* views. The teacher has her opportunity to teach in the wrap-up.)

Affirm and Encourage

The single most important rule to remember in leading a discussion is to acknowledge every comment in a positive way. You encourage or discourage the women to present their ideas by the way you respond to their remarks. Even if a woman says, "The moon is made out of green cheese," you can answer, "Thank you for telling us your idea." To say, "I don't agree" or to ignore the remark is to convey rejection.

Affirm the woman herself when you cannot agree with her thoughts. She has studied the lesson; she's made the effort to come to class; she needs encouragement to go on learning.

Be aware that body language (gestures and facial expressions) also conveys approval or disapproval. Always display warmth and graciousness.

Unscriptural Answers

It will sometimes be necessary to field a theologically incorrect answer. *No matter how unscriptural an observation may be, the leader must maintain her position of neutrality and accept the opinion offered.* She cannot step out of her role as discussion guide to "straighten out" a woman whose notions do not hold with the mainstream of Christian teaching. It would be dishonest to state that in a discussion all opinions can be voiced, then be unreceptive to differing ideas. The way to handle a biblically unsound answer is to acknowledge it pleasantly and positvely, then call for further discussion. Someone in the group will have enough knowledge of Scripture to present God's view of the issue.

You may at first question the wisdom of allowing unscriptural ideas to pass unchecked, fearing it may cause confusion in the minds of women who do not have a firm grasp on biblical principles. But remember that the Holy Spirit is present as "the Teacher" and can be trusted to help class members sort through the ideas they hear. And the wrap-up that follows the discussion hour brings truth into focus for them.

SETTING: The discussion group.

QUESTION: *In Colossians 2, Paul warns against mysticism and the worship of angels (v. 18) and tells his readers not to believe they can please God by keeping rules and rituals (vv. 20-23). What do you think Paul meant when he called rules and rituals a "shadow"?*

Marilyn: "Barbara, what do you think Paul meant by a 'shadow'?"

Barbara: "I guess he meant that it didn't have substance. A shadow is a picture or a reflection of something real and solid.

"This whole passage interests me, especially the part concerning angels. I've read a lot about UFO's (Unidentified Flying Objects), and I think that what we call angels are actually astronauts from outer space. People in Paul's day were less educated, so if they saw a man from another planet, they would naturally think he was some supernatural being worthy of worship."

Marilyn: "You're not alone in your belief. I've heard other people say they equate angels with astronauts. Have you ever done an in-depth study of angels as the Bible presents them? I think it would be interesting to compare the teachings of Scripture with the books you've been reading.

"Barbara, I like your description of a shadow as being a reflection of something else. You've given us a good start on this question.

"Janet, what do *you* think Paul meant when he referred to rules and regulations as shadows?"

SETTING: The discussion group.

QUESTION: *In Colossians 2, Paul warns against philosophies that can lead Christians away from a vital relationship with Christ. Have you ever followed a philosophy (perhaps a religious one) that was based on man's thinking, not God's? What did you learn from this experience?*

Pat: "Why is a philosophy or a religion based on man's thinking necessarily bad? I studied comparative religions in college and came to the conclusion that mankind has learned many ways to find truth and, ultimately, God. I think Christians are too narrow-minded when they say that believing in Christ and following the Bible is the only way to know God."

Marilyn: "Thank you for giving us your viewpoint, Pat. We don't want to overlook the fact that every religion has good points.

"Who else has thought about this question and would like to discuss it?"

Marge: "Before I became a Christian, I investigated other religions. I even followed a guru and learned Transcendental Meditation. The problem I found was that meditating and seeking wisdom wasn't satisfying. Then one day a friend told me that through Christ I could be personally related to God. I prayed to receive Christ as Savior and since then have experienced peace of mind and a sense of purpose in life. Never have I regretted becoming a Christian. What I do regret are the years I wasted looking for a 'religious experience.' "

Marilyn: "Thank you, Marge, for giving your testimony. I, too, discovered that there is a vast difference between

Christianity and other religions, which is why I chose to become a Christian.

"Would someone else like to talk about this question?"

When a leader handles a "wrong" answer in a tactful way, the group member continues to feel accepted and doesn't hesitate to answer another question.

Maintaining Control

Because time is limited, it is necessary that a group leader exercise sufficient control to (1) keep the discussion centered on the questions and (2) cut off problem talkers. The Discussion Guidelines given below have been reprinted in the appendix so the leader can cut them out and have them reproduced. A copy of these guidelines then can be given to each member the first week she attends the class. This will help maintain the control necessary since the leader can refer the group to the guidelines whenever she needs to remind them of the principles of good discussion.

DISCUSSION GUIDELINES

1. Come to class prepared. You will have more to offer if you have answered your questions thoroughly and have thought through the subjects covered in the lesson.

2. Share your knowledge. Your insights and experiences are different from those of every other class member. Allow them to benefit from what only you can offer.

3. Do not wait to be called on. If you wait, you may forget what you want to say, or you may miss the most appropriate time to say it.

4. Keep your comments related to the conversation. Time is limited, and it's important to cover the assigned topics.
5. Listen thoughtfully. Try to understand the other person's point of view. Maintain an open mind.
6. Be considerate. Check yourself to see if you are talking more than anyone else. Give others a chance to participate.
7. Do not expect the group leader to correct someone you think has the "wrong" answer. (She will not "correct" you, either, if your opinion is different from others expressed). The leader's function is to facilitate the discussion, not to draw out one specific answer on each question.
8. ABOVE ALL, HAVE FUN! Enjoy the discussion!

Balancing Participation

Most women show consideration for others and do not dominate conversations. But some like to talk . . . and talk . . . and talk. They can carry on a monologue on any subject at any time, not realizing that their audience isn't as interested in listening as they are in talking. Occasionally one of these women joins a Bible class. How does the leader handle her?

If one person dominates a discussion, you can take control by calling on someone to answer each question. The volunteer system won't work in this case. If in spite of your efforts the talker gains momentum, graciously and tactfully say, "Although this is interesting, our time together is short, and we have other subjects to cover. We should move on." Being cut off a few times will show her that her comments need to be more concise. It also boosts the morale of the group. When one person is allowed to ramble, other women begin to feel restless or annoyed. *The leader considers the good of the entire group* and controls the talker.

In contrast to the marathon talker is the shy or overly quiet woman. Because she is easy to overlook, you will want to make a special effort to draw her out. Call on her to answer very simple questions, or solicit her help in planning a group coffee. Give her a little extra attention, and she will feel an essential part of the group.

The Expert

A few discussion group participants feel compelled to correct the answers of those who have less biblical knowledge or do not see the value of living by scriptural principles. Usually their theology is right; their attitude is the problem. To have a group member offended because she has been "jumped on" verbally is to lose her from the class. The leader must affirm *both* women ("We appreciate hearing your views"), but she must restrain the expert. She might say, "It's obvious that our opinions will differ, because we have different backgrounds and varying degrees of biblical understanding. It's not important that we agree totally."

Another approach is to refer everyone back to the lesson with a comment such as, "We seem to be getting somewhat sidetracked. Let's return to the lesson." Then quickly *call on* someone to answer the next question.

Sometimes the leader needs to talk frankly with the expert outside the class. Invite her for coffee, or treat her to lunch. Let her know how much you appreciate her for who she is and for the depth of knowledge she contributes to the discussion each week. Tactfully point out, however, that being corrected publicly is embarrassing. Solict her help in making the less knowledgeable women feel comfortable in the group.

Eye Contact

Maintain good eye contact at all times. Do not fall into the habit of looking down at your question sheet. Direct your attention to the group, and look at your paper *only* when reading a question aloud.

The Visitor

When you have a first-time visitor or a new attendee who has not seen the questions in advance, give her the opportunity to participate by asking her to read Bible verses or relate her experiences on the personal opinion questions. Encourage her to return the following week with her questions answered, so she will have more to contribute. Do not solicit off-the-cuff answers from those who have not prepared the lesson.

Discussing Problems

As you lead, be sensitive to women with problems. If a question or comment reveals that a group member is struggling in some area, and if discussing her problem would be of value to others, very tactfully pursue the point. Do not pursue it if the subject is not of general interest or value. (Topics of interest might be: children, marital problems, witnessing. Avoid discussing details of family illnesses, problems with pets, and gossip picked up at the beauty shop.)

SETTING: The discussion group.

QUESTION: Paul indicates that how Christians think is important (Col. 3:1, 2). Being honest with yourself, make note of what you spend the most time thinking about. Is this the subject that should occupy the center of your thoughts? Why or why not?

Marilyn: "This is another personal question. I never call on anyone to answer this type of question because it is so personal. At this point we need volunteers."

Silence. No volunteers.

Marilyn: "This question made me aware of some things about myself. After reading Colossians 3, I knew that Christ should be in the center of my thoughts, and I realized that recently He hasn't been. When I examined my thought patterns, I found that the thing I'm preoccupied with is worry about my teenage daughter. She's been running a low-grade fever and seems tired and listless. Our family doctor doesn't think it's serious, but I find my mind returning to her again and again. I pray but can't seem to trust God enough to stop worrying. I'd appreciate it if all of you would pray with me."

Marge: "It makes me feel better to hear you say you worry, too. Sometimes I get so obsessed with worrying I wonder if I'm really a Christian. Studying Colossians has helped me see how I can change some of my thought patterns. I think this is the best lesson we've had all year."

Marilyn: "I feel the same way, Marge. I needed this lesson.

"Would someone else like to comment on the subject of our thoughts?"

Joy: "I would. Maybe you can help me with a problem I'm having. I dream a lot and spend hours trying to figure out what they mean. I have one recurring dream about going to a dinner-dance. I always wear a sequined dress and pile my hair on top of my head like a fashion model. The first person I meet at the party is my old college roommate who says, 'Let's get out of this stuffy place and go to the beach.' I've had this dream so many times I know what she's going to say before she says it.

"Can you tell me what this dream means? I know some people can interpret these things."

Marilyn: "I'm sorry, Joy, but how to interpret dreams is a little outside the scope of a Bible class. I don't think anyone here is qualified to draw conclusions about your dreams. If you find an answer, we'd be interested in hearing about it.

"Is everyone ready to move on to the next question?"

Janet: "I'd like to talk about *this* question. I've been a Christian a long time, and I've learned *how* to keep Christ in the center of my thoughts; I just don't do it consistently. When I fail the most is when my husband and I have an argument. I don't know what's wrong, but the past few weeks we've disagreed several times. Nothing serious, but it bothers me. I get upset and my problems occupy my mind more than Christ does. I wish I could get myself under control."

Marilyn: "I think all of us have gone through something similar. I know I have."

Kay: "Is it possible that your husband is under pressure at work? Usually when my husband and I get into arguments, it's because he's edgy about something at the office."

Nancy: "Have you thought about seeing a counselor? A while back my husband and I had a disagreement and I talked to our pastor. He helped me to understand some of our basic problems. I'm strong-willed, and I don't let my husband make decisions without challenging his authority. It wasn't easy to be told I was causing most of the friction, and it was even harder to apologize to my husband, but it improved our marriage."

Barbara: "Talking to a close friend helps me to put things in perspective."

Janet: "I guess I haven't talked to anyone until now because of pride. I don't like to admit that anything bothers me."

Marilyn: "It takes courage to talk about our problems. Is there anything we can do to help? Please tell us if there is."

Janet: "You've helped already. I guess I needed to hear that other people struggle with the same things I do."

Marilyn prepared the way for Marge and Janet to discuss their anxieties by voicing her worry over her daughter. The resulting conversation was beneficial to several women. Marilyn did not allow the group to be drawn into Joy's "problem," because speculating about dreams would not be profitable or consistent with the goals of the class.

Different answers must be handled in different ways. This takes expertise the leader can gain only through practice. Reading about leading a group won't turn anyone into a leader; she must actually step out and do it. She gains skill week by week as she practices the principles of good discussion with her group.

A good discussion leader also seizes every opportunity to promote conversation *outside* the class. Family members appreciate her good listening habits and positive response to their remarks. Friends sense her intense interest when they offer their ideas because she asks perceptive questions. Casual acquaintances enjoy responding to queries such as, "How do *you* feel about the weather, your job, the new fashions, the headlines, the changes in the community?" Everyone is cheered by hearing her say, "I've enjoyed talking with you; you've made my day more interesting."

6

Susan's Story

"I really enjoyed that," Ginny told Ann one morning after hearing the wrap-up. "Susan speaks so naturally and easily."

Ann agreed. "I wish I had her talent. She always seems to know just what I'm thinking and speaks directly to me."

Ginny and Ann would be surprised to learn that speaking did not come easily for Susan. Her ability developed through hard work and practice. In fact, Susan never planned to be a speaker. She had joined the Bible class as a participant five years earlier and would have laughed had anyone predicted she would eventually teach the group.

Susan discovered the Bible study the fall her youngest child entered kindergarten. For the first time in years, her schedule was freer. In the supermarket she noticed a poster advertising the class and thought, *Why not give it a try?* Soon she was engrossed in Bible study and involved in the lives of the women in her discussion group. Because of her enthusiasm and her caring attitude, she was invited to train as a group leader.

The next two years were spent leading her discussion group and learning more about the Bible. Those years were life-changing. In writing to her mother after her first six months as a leader, she said,

Dear Mom,

I must tell you what has been happening to me in the Bible class. It's just too good to keep to myself.

When I became a leader, I felt totally inadequate (I still do most of the time), but it's amazing what God has done! First of all, I've learned to pray; I mean *really* pray! My past catch-as-catch-can, on-the-run prayers seem so inadequate now. I take time each morning to talk to God and to sit in His presence to listen for the still, small voice of the Holy Spirit. I've come to know my Father in heaven in a way I didn't imagine I *could* know Him. I always envied the very "real" prayers you pray; now I'm beginning to understand what you knew that I didn't.

And I've learned a lot about listening. Our leaders' training manual stresses the importance of keeping an open, receptive ear to everyone. As a new leader I reminded myself every class day, *Now listen well!! The girls in your group have important things to say!* Gradually, without realizing how the change came about, I "caught myself" being a listener not just on Wednesday morning, but on every other day as well. It has become a habit, a real part of *me*, to hear things even Joe and the kids tell me. And I've discovered what fascinating neighbors and friends I have! How much I missed by only half-listening to conversations!

Being a Bible class leader has been stretching but fun! I can't begin to describe the closeness in the leader's group. We work together, pray together and laugh a lot. The fellowship is wonderful!

Mom, I woke up this morning thinking about you. I owe you so much. You and Dad led me to Christ and instilled in me a love for Scripture. One reason I'm enjoying this ministry is that you started me in this direction years ago.

Gratefully,
Susan

As she continued to lead her group, Susan's knowledge of the Bible expanded, and she became increasingly sensitive to the needs of the women in the class. Many of them did not have her advantages: Christian parents, a loving husband, and healthy children. Often she heard such things as "My husband is having an affair with his secretary," or "My child has an incurable illness," or "I don't know why but I feel restless and dissatisfied most of the time." Again and again Susan knelt to ask God's guidance in how to respond to needs and hurts. She encouraged her women to apply biblical principles to their problems, and her own life modeled the results of living as the Bible teaches.

One morning Susan received a call from Mary, the teacher who presented the wrap-up each week. Mary's husband was being transferred to another state, and they would be moving soon. Would Susan consent to be the new teacher? Susan's reaction was a mixture of pleasure and panic.

"I'm honored you would ask me," she said, "but I don't consider myself a teacher. My only experience has been teaching children in Sunday school and the practice wrap-ups we do in the leaders' meetings. I enjoy discussing my thoughts with the other leaders, but it scares me to think about speaking to the entire class."

Mary answered, "Every group leader is trained to do wrap-ups for a reason! If a teacher leaves, someone should be ready to step into her shoes. You are the one I hope to see teaching when I move. Please pray about it and discuss it with Joe, and I'll call you again in a few days."

That evening after the children were in bed, Susan and Joe talked over coffee and dessert.

Susan explained what would be entailed in teaching: extra hours of study and an investment in additional books, as well as increased responsibility. She didn't want to short-change her family by taking on more than she could reasonably handle.

Joe's analysis of the situation surprised Susan. "Up to this point your participation in the class has been nothing but positive. You seem happier and aren't thrown off stride by things that used to upset you. How can additional Bible study be anything but beneficial?

"Frankly, I like what's happened to you in the class. I'm especially impressed with the way you relate to people since you began leaders' training. You used to be a little uncomfortable with the guys from the office who are not Christians. Remember all the excuses you made to avoid office parties? Now you reach out to people who may never have contact with Christians other than us. I like that. And I'd like to see you help others learn to do the same.

"Sure, you may have to give up some things you enjoy to make more time for preparing wrap-ups, but think of the many women who will benefit from your presentation."

As Joe spoke, the Holy Spirit seemed to impress on Susan, "It's your turn. You are prepared to take Mary's place. You can trust Me to work through you as I worked through her."

A study on spiritual gifts (in 1 Cor. 12—14) reinforced Susan's thinking. She recognized her God-given ability to teach and thanked God for it. Later, in speaking to the class, she said, "A spiritual gift fits each of us into a special ministry within the Body of Christ. It equips us for the unique task God has chosen for us. Many women say they will never reach their highest potential without a career or a large paycheck, but nothing could be more fulfilling to me than serving my Creator in the job He created me to do!"

Susan's teaching ability blossomed as she applied good study habits and depended on the Holy Spirit to give her fresh inspirational ideas for each week's presentation. The telephone was unplugged each morning (although some days she couldn't free the entire two hours she planned) as she delved into the Bible and related reading. Every wrap-up was written, rewritten, and bathed in prayer. Sometimes while shopping, or in the middle of the night, creative ideas popped into her mind as the fruit of study and prayer came together.

In teaching the class, Susan often related what she learned about herself as she studied God's Word. Her audience loved hearing the specifics of these spiritual lessons. Anecdotes from her reading did not make as great an impact as a simple illustration from her own experience. She never represented herself as "having arrived", but as a fellow-pilgrim in the Christian life.

The rewards of teaching were many. Susan benefited daily from the discipline of her self-imposed study routine. It taught her to be efficient in each day's activities and to cut out nonessentials. Also, her spiritual life deepened. Being responsible for teaching others motivated her to know and *obey* God's Word herself. Her greatest joy was seeing changes in the lives of women like Ginny.

Ginny became a Christian under Susan's teaching and progressed rapidly in her understanding of the Bible. And everything she learned she applied. Her changed life witnessed to the reality of her experience with Christ.

7
Teaching the Wrap-Up

Preparing and delivering the wrap-up is never dull.

Women like Susan give their lives to teaching the Bible and find it not only worthwhile, but also extremely interesting. From Genesis to Revelation, this ancient document is fascinating to read and study. It grips the mind and imagination with the freshness of the morning newspaper. Today's journalists report on presidents and politicians and the way men of power conduct themselves. So does Scripture. Read the Old Testament books of First and Second Kings, and imagine the biographies of the kings in a modern setting. These historical accounts are as relevant today as they were when they were written.

Scan the scenario of David and Bathsheba with a reporter's eye (2 Sam. 11, 12). This scandal would make the front page of every newspaper in the country. Headlines would scream: "KING GUILTY OF ADULTERY AND MURDER!" The text would go on to relate David's deadly plot against his neighbor, Uriah, the outgrowth of his lust for Uriah's wife.

The financial section of the paper might record the rags-to-riches story of a man like Joseph (Gen. 37—45). Joseph was an unknown Hebrew lad, sold into slavery by his jealous brothers. When he later rose to become second in command to the Pharoah of Egypt, his fame spread throughout the known world.

Women readers would be captivated with the profile of Queen Esther (Old Testament book of Esther). Her story has intrigue and romance; it was love at first sight for the king. The queen used her beauty, intelligence and courage to influence the course of history.

The Bible speaks in an absorbing and authoritative manner on many subjects: politics, human rights, business, marriage, sex, money, and ecology, to name just a few. The examples of everyday living from the Old Testament, the life of Christ in the Gospels, the birth of Christianity in the book of Acts, and the letters to the churches can be studied again and again. Each time they seem new and interesting. It's impossible to exhaust the depth and meaning of the Bible.

It is not necessary to be a scholar, however, to understand its content. It was written to be understood by the average man and woman.

You may have begun reading this book with a hesitancy about teaching a Bible class because you do not have an in-depth knowledge of Scripture, or because you are afraid you will misinterpret its meaning. When that hesitancy recurs, remember that long before there were scholars of theology or printed study aids, Christians were studying and teaching God's Word. Do not take liberties in teaching, be as accurate as possible, but be aware that the Bible was addressed to the common man, not theologians. It is a practical book that speaks to the real issues Christians face every day.

Preparing the Message

Step One: Analysis

The first step in preparing a wrap-up of twenty-five minutes is to analyze the passage to be taught. Most of the analysis is done while charting the chapter and writing discussion questions, although details may need to be explored further. For instance, it is helpful to look into the background of the people and the places mentioned in the text, the conditions under which the passage was written, and the meaning of difficult words and phrases.

Example from Colossians

This section is included because many years of training discussion leaders and teachers has taught me that women want not only the "how to" of message preparation, but also specific examples.

As indicated in chapter 4, "(Developing the Lesson"), Colossians 3:1—4:1 was researched in the process of writing questions. I read through this passage in several different translations of the Bible. I checked a Bible dictionary for definitions of words like "submission" and "love" to be sure I had grasped their correct meaning.

Next, I re-read the passage paragraph by paragraph and made notes in columns titled "Summary," "Application," and "Discussion Questions."

Finally, I referred to commentaries for historical information and to compare my work with the writings of authors who have extensive background in the Greek language. (Making this comparison part of my study routine gives me a broader view of Scripture and tells me if I have wandered afield in interpreting the passage. Experience has taught me that my viewpoint may differ from that of the commentator because my mental grid is different, but there should not be conflict. If there is, I re-study and re-think my original ideas.)

Step Two: Selection of a Theme

An easy-to-follow, easy-to-apply message will have one main theme or central idea. Step 2 in preparation is choosing the theme and stating it in one or two crisp, concise sentences.

Most chapters of the Bible touch on several subjects (themes). Some themes are dominant and can be considered major ideas, while others are minor. Look for both in each chapter you study.

As you select a biblical theme to develop, consider the needs of your audience. Will you be speaking primarily to career women excited about their jobs? Will your hearers be young mothers exhausted by the responsibility of caring for small children? Are all Christians or are some not Christians? How much do they already know about the Bible? Learn as much as possible about the women in your class, and choose a theme that will fit their needs and interests.

Example from Colossians

Colossians 3:1—4:1 contains a number of subjects that would appeal to women in Bible classes. As I analyzed this section of Scripture, I saw three main (interconnected) themes. (1) Our thought patterns reflect our relationship with Christ (3:1-4); (2) our behavior patterns reflect our relationship with Christ (3:5-17); and (3) our relationships with people reflect our relationship with Christ (3:18—4:1).

All three themes could be used in one wrap-up, but none could be developed fully within the time frame. Since the classes I teach are composed mostly of young to middle-aged women who consider family members and friends the most important people in their lives, I chose to develop the section on relationships (our relationships with people reflect our relationship with Christ).

Had I wished to narrow my subject further, I could have moved from the broad theme of relationships into one specific area. For instance, Colossians 3:18 would lend itself to the topic: "A woman who is rightly related to Christ will submit to her husband" or "A woman's relationship with Christ is reflected in her attitudes and actions toward her husband."

An audience can remember and be motivated to use one clearly presented, well-developed theme. Covering too much territory or too many ideas will ensure that most of the message is forgotten.

It is not necessary to include every part of the chapter in the presentation, as class members study the passage verse-by-verse in answering their questions. More of an impact is made by broadening their thinking in one area.

Step Three: A Basic Outline

A message is outlined by organizing the facts and ideas contained in the passage to be taught. Just as the theme comes from Scriptures, so does the outline. The verses that shape the theme also shape the outline.

Example from Colossians

    Theme: Our relationships with people reflect our relationship with Christ.

    Introduction: Behind every action is a motivation. The best motive is a desire to please God (3:17, 23).

    I. Relationships motivated by desire to please God reflect Christ-like attitudes and actions (3:18—4:1):

      1. Wives submit to their husbands.
      2. Husbands love their wives.
      3. Children obey their parents.
      4. Parents do not provoke their children.
      5. Servants obey their masters.
      6. Masters treat their servants fairly.

    II. Relationships that reflect Christ-like attitudes and actions earn eternal rewards (3:23-25).

Step Four: An Expanded Outline

From a bare-bones outline as described in step 3, an expanded outline can be sketched. As you rework an outline, plan to restate the central theme (several times, if possible). Explain the theme, support it, illustrate it, and apply it. Draw in related passages of Scripture, ideas gained from current events, or pertinent background material.

Example from Colossians

As I begin filling in an outline I ask myself. *What will my audience want to know about this passage of Scripture? What questions will it raise in their minds?* I do not necessarily include the questions themselves in the finished wrap-up, but they guide the selection of material that goes into the presentation.

If I am dealing with the subject of submission, I consider, "What is submission? How does it reflect a woman's relationship with Christ? What objections might my audience have to being taught submission?"

As I think through a husband's responsibility to love his wife, I ask, "What is love? How does it reflect Christ-likeness? What happens if a man does not understand or is not willing to practice love as the Bible teaches it?"

Knowing the questions I want to answer tells me where the outline needs additional support and which ideas need to be illustrated to become clear and applicable. The basic outline of Colossians 3:18, 19 might be reworked this way.

I. Relationships motivated by desire to please God reflect Christ-like attitudes and actions.

1. A wife reflects her relationship to Christ when she submits to her husband.

   a. Submission means willingly yielding in love. A wife voluntarily accepts her husband's authority.

   b. Submission is for today because the Bible is for today.

   c. Submission reflects Christ-likeness. He submitted to His Father (Phil. 2:5—8).

2. A husband reflects his relationship with Christ when he loves his wife.

   a. Love means seeking the best for the other person. The Bible always equates loving with giving.

   b. Love reflects Christ-likeness because it is self-sacrificing (John 3:16 and 15:13).

c. Some men do not understand or do not practice love as the Bible teaches it. Their wives can display Christ-like love to them (1 Pet. 3:1).

Step Five: The Written Message

A rough draft comes next. In drafting the talk word-for-word, flesh is added to the skeleton of the outline. The writer becomes a storyteller, filling in details that make the message come alive in the minds of the hearers.

When you write a wrap-up, use your outline as your guide. If it contains a logical progression of ideas, so will your message. (If the outline does not help you maintain a clear train of thought, go back and revise it.)

Write your wrap-up as if you are talking directly to someone. In your mind, address a friend sitting across the table from you. Explain your message to her in the same words you would use in normal conversation.

Pay particular attention to the transitions—the way you go from point A to point B. If your talk seems ragged or jerky, the problem may lie with the transitions.

Consider your introduction and conclusion carefully. An introduction is designed to capture attention and get your audience thinking along with you. A conclusion finishes and completes. It ends a talk at the right time and in the most effective manner. It leaves your listeners challenged and motivated to apply the truths you've taught.

Your manuscript may need to be rewritten several times before it acquires the polish you desire, but the end result will justify the extra time and work.

Example from Colossians

The finished wrap-up for Colossians 3:1—4:1 is included with the section on Colossians at the end of the book.

Step Six: Rehearsal

The final step in message preparation is rehearsal. The written talk must become so familiar that it is easy to deliver. The key is repetition.

Read the entire message aloud several times. You will remember more if you've heard it as well as read it.

Tape the message and play it back as you work in the house or drive the car. Hearing it this way will tell you if the flow is good, if you've made your ideas clear, and if you sound enthusiastic. (Your audience won't be excited about your talk if you are not.)

Rehearse in front of a mirror. Check to see if you have distracting mannerisms or if you need more facial expression. Practice smiling. When you look happy, your listeners feel at ease and know you enjoy talking to them. Remember, you are not "giving a speech," you are communicating from your heart to theirs.

You will feel less need to depend on notes if you digest your message thoroughly. Don't memorize! Concentrate on the flow of ideas, not the exact working.

Assignment: Complete a Wrap-Up

While this chapter is fresh in your mind, try your hand at writing a wrap-up. In chapter 4 you were given the assignment of writing a set of discussion questions. Use the same passage of Scripture you chose for the questions, and follow these steps now to a completed message:

STEP ONE: Review the analysis (chart) you did of the passage.

STEP TWO: Pick out several themes (major and minor, broad and narrow) from the passage of Scripture. Select one main idea to develop into a talk.

STEP THREE: Shape an outline using the verses from which you selected your theme. By taking the outline from Scripture, your message will follow the logical progression of ideas presented in the passage.

STEP FOUR: Expand your outline. As you did background study for writing questions, you stockpiled many ideas that can be brought into the wrap-up. Amplify your outline by making brief note of some of these ideas. Add Scripture verses that support your theme. Mark the places appropriate for illustrations.

In expanding your outline, remember that your aim is to motivate the audience to act on the principles you present. Make clear what actions you are recommending and how to implement them.

STEP FIVE: Draft your message. Give it shape and form by rounding out the thoughts sketched in the outline. By writing out a complete message, you will know exactly what you want to say and how best to say it.

STEP SIX: Polish and rehearse your message, then find a place to use it. If you have not yet begun a Bible class, volunteer to speak at a ladies' luncheon or a neighborhood coffee. Every time you stand in front of an audience, you will gain experience and poise. Teaching a Bible class will be just a step away.

8
Starting the Class

Through the eyes of Ginny (chap. 1) and Susan (chap. 6), you have seen a large Bible discussion class that meets in a church and touches an entire city. But this is only one type of class incorporating the use of Bible discussion methods. The basic principles of study, lesson development, teaching and leadership training can be varied in their application. The variations encompass studies with no wrap-up and groups that use sets of question obtained from books, although *all* classes use written questions requiring home study and discussion participation. A sampling of existing discussion groups would disclose applications such as:

Small groups meeting in homes. Attendees are neighbors who live on the block.

Bible discussion groups gathered on college campuses and military bases.

Classes formed around special interests such as medicine, law or the arts. Team-teaching is often used with these career-oriented classes. A heavy work schedule may prevent one person from committing to teach every week all year. But two or more teachers can each present one series in the course of a year.

Bible discussion groups for office workers held during lunch hour. Because of time limitations, there is usually no wrap-up.

Evening classes for men. Pioneers of these classes are, for the most part, husbands of women in daytime studies. These men appreciate the benefits of the class because of the changes they see in their wives.

Church-sponsored classes for teenagers that consist of discussion groups followed by wrap-up. Discussion questions come from Christian publications geared to teens. High school students lead the discussion and conduct the leaders' meeting. Group sponsors, church staff, or special guests deliver the wrap-up.

Adult Sunday school classes that discuss the same passage of Scripture the pastor uses as his sermon text. Discussion questions are written by the pastor and printed in the bulletin a week ahead.

Although each of these classes differs in operational details, all have one thing in common; they began in response to a *need*. Sometimes the need was for one woman to introduce her friend to Bible study. At other times the need was shared concern for a community. One class began after fifty women met to pray, asking God to send them a Bible teacher. Within weeks a trained Bible discussion leader moved into the area and a class was formed. More than one hundred women attended the first session. Other classes started as spin-offs of larger groups. As a class grew to the capacity of a facility, several leaders and class members from a common area of the city opted to "spin-off" and form a class in their own neighborhood.

In your area, you may be the person who feels the need or sees the potential for a class. You may live in a small town or a large city. Your part of the country may be traditional and slow to accept new ideas, or it may be sophisticated and eager for fresh concepts. The general population may consist of singles, young families or retirees. Wherever you reside, Bible discussion groups can be adapted to your locality and its special needs.

Who Will Come

How do you actually begin a class? You start by thinking "friends." Whose lives do you touch—neighbors, business associates, teenagers? Because of your interests, your personality, or your particular set of circumstances, there are those who will be drawn to you, and through you into God's Word. Build relationships. Get to know your neighbors. Join *secular* organizations. (Many Christians stick together, witnessing and teaching the Bible to each other rather than reaching the non-Christian world with the message of Christ). In all your contacts, consider the future as well as the present. Remember that the person you meet today may be influenced for Christ a year from now.

As you make contacts, ask the Holy Spirit to lead you to the person who can help you in praying for and planning a class. One of the reasons God places Christians in a community of believers is to give them support and encouragement. It's hard to hold onto a dream alone. Keep your spiritual antennae out for a fellow-dreamer, someone who sees the same need you do and can work with you toward fulfilling that dream. Assign her the title of class coordinator or administrative assistant, and include her in all the arrangements for the class.

Developing Material

In the weeks and months you are planning and praying, be preparing Bible study material. Set aside time each day to read God's Word and chart it as outlined in chapter 4. Ask your assistant to do the same; then review and evaluate each other's notes. Consider who will be answering the questions as you decide which ones to include in the finished lesson. (Teenagers need a different emphasis than middle-aged women, for example.) With a little practice you will grasp the knack of compiling discussion questions.

Later, after your class is established and you are in the process of training additional leaders, you may find several women who enjoy writing questions and can contribute material for lessons. Occasionally you might use a series from among the books of printed questions available in Christian bookstores. (This will entail each class member's buying a booklet.) But a word of caution concerning the use of outside material: of necessity it is more general and less personal. The author has not met the women in your class and does not know the particular subjects they need to discuss in depth. Developing your own skill in writing questions gives you the most options; it frees you from dependence on outside sources, yet gives you the choice of using published material well-suited to your group.

Inviting Participants

With lessons ready and a few friends to be invited, set a date to begin the class, and start spreading the word. It may be easiest to make phone calls, but it's more effective to place an invitation in someone's hand. The invitation should include basic information such as the date, time, place, and topic for study. It should name the person who will be leading the class and mention that the group is inter-denominational. (Prospective class members need to know you are not trying to draw them into your church or denomination.) If you provide a nursery, this should be mentioned. A phone number can be listed for further information.

Shape this information into attractive posters to clip to the bulletin board in the supermarket or laundromat. Mimeograph flyers to hand out in your neighborhood. Carry a few invitations in your purse, and give them to acquaintances you meet while shopping or chauffeuring the children to school. Spread your invitations widely with a prayer that God will draw in the women He wants to attend. He will.

Introducing the Class

As the women gather in your home or church, greet each one warmly, thank her for coming, introduce her to others, and serve her tea or coffee and a slice of homemade cake. After a short period of socializing, call the group together and experience the thrill of introducing a new Bible class, perhaps the first Bible discussion group in your area.

Begin your presentation by putting your audience at ease. Re-state your joy at seeing each one present. Verbalize your happy anticipation at the prospect of studying the Bible with them. Use every word and every gesture to build rapport.

Explain in detail how the class functions. The women will already know you are introducing a Bible class and may be aware it combines home study, discussion and a teaching session, but they need the details of the class set-up.

Explain that study questions will be distributed each week. Give some hints on how to answer the questions. Highlight the importance of individual study and the benefits to be received.

Detail how the discussion groups work, who will lead them and how to participate. Be motivational in your approach—talk about the fun of pooling information and sharing personal insights.

Tell the group what the wrap-up is designed to accomplish (i.e., tie the lesson together and give specific ways the passage of Scripture can be applied.)

Your talk should also cover information such as how the nursery workers are paid (voluntary contributions). If your class meets in a church, a monetary gift should be given to the church periodically as a "thank you" for the use of the facilities.

At this point in your introduction, you may want to present (1) a personal testimony or (2) an introduction to the book of the Bible selected for study. Choose the type of presentation your particular audience will benefit from the most.

Personal Testimony. Nothing is more appealing to women than a personal testimony. Describing your background and experience helps a group to know you and relate to you. Include in your testimony the story of how you first became interested in a Bible class. Communicate excitement about the Bible by telling what Bible study has meant to you. (Was your life changed by studying and applying God's Word? Was your family affected? Were problems solved? Are you happier or more able to cope because you live by biblical principles?)

Introduction to a book of the Bible. In preparing sets of discussion questions, you will have gathered much background material on the book designated for study. Pass on some of your knowledge. Explain who wrote the book, when it was written, the purpose, the main themes, and other information you deem interesting.

Your discourse should be challenging, creative and designed to capture the imagination of the audience. Do not rely on facts alone (Paul *went* here and *did* this), but include a personality profile of the writer of the book or of a character who appears in the book.

One fascinating way to present background information is to do it in the first person. ("My name is Ruth. A godly mother-in-law named Naomi and a little town called Bethlehem have figured largely in my life. Let me tell you about it.") Role-playing the life of a biblical character is fun both for the one who does the portrayal and for those who listen. Women never forget what they hear from a biblical figure who steps out of the pages of history to speak directly to them.

At the close of your delivery, hand out discussion questions for the next week. Stand near the door as the women depart, and give each one a friendly word.

Breathe a prayer of thanks and a sigh of relief! Your class is launched!

9

Training the Leaders

Envision a few of your friends and acquaintances sitting in a circle, Bibles and lesson sheets on their laps. Picture the group in animated discussion, led by the person who has assisted you in preparing for the class. See yourself giving the wrap-up at the close of the discussion hour.

The typical Bible discussion class begins with two leaders, one to lead the discussion (a group leader) and one to deliver the wrap-up (the teacher). As the class grows, additional leaders are added and trained. This chapter provides a teacher's guide to selecting and training group leaders. A format for the leaders' meeting is included.

Choosing Leaders

Leaders do not just "happen"; their selection and training is important. To select leaders, look for women who are growing spiritually and whose lives exhibit the characteristics outlined in chapter 3.

Some women attend a Bible class to gain intellectual knowledge or to enjoy the fellowship. They are marvelous participants but should not be considered for leadership. Choose as leaders women who are faithful in attendance, who do their questions consistently, and who are excited about being Christians. Given time to mature, a participant who becomes a Christian through the class often makes an excellent leader. Because she has been helped by the class, she is enthusiastic about being in a position to help others.

Even in a class of only twelve or fifteen women, there will probably be one you want to train as a group leader. Talk with her about the goals and responsibilities of leadership, and invite her to join you and your assistant for each week's leaders' meeting. Adding her to the group helps you prepare for future growth. It is always best to have trainee leaders in reserve so as not to be caught short if the class grows quickly or loses a leader.

The Leaders' Meeting

The leaders' meeting has two purposes: to make advance preparation for the class, and to train leaders. (If this is your first experience in directing a Bible class, the leaders' meeting will be on-the-job training for you as well.) Leaders pray together, go over the lesson for the next class, and practice fielding a discussion. Periodically they prepare and deliver a practice wrap-up.

The leaders' meeting is held at the time most convenient for the leaders. When a class meets in the morning, leaders' training generally follows. It begins with lunch and a review of the morning's activities, then progresses into prayer and instruction. Leaders who work with evening groups often choose to meet before the class. They bring a sandwich and enjoy a period of informal fellowship before turning their thoughts to Bible study. The time you choose for your leaders' meeting will depend on the needs and desires of your group.

Because the leaders' meeting is the training ground for leaders, it's vital to make the best possible use of the time you have together. From the very first, establish an orderly pattern that will accomplish the most in an efficient manner. The following segments should be included in the meeting. Each segment has been assigned a suggested time allotment to demonstrate that all essentials can be covered in less than two hours.

Review (10 minutes)

Begin with a short review and evaluation of the previous class. This will tell you if you need to do something differently for the next class. Discuss what went well. Ask, "What could be improved?" and "What needs did you notice among the women in your group?"

Prayer (20 minutes)

A Bible class is God's class and does not go forward without His blessing. Prayer reminds leaders to be totally dependent on Him.

Prayer in the leaders' meeting is specific. It concentrates on the women in the class, the community you want to reach for Christ, the leaders and their family members. (These are the areas of common interest, and time is too short to cover a wide range of requests.)

Conversational prayer is utilized. Even women who are not accustomed to praying aloud find this type of prayer uncomplicated and easy to practice. In praying conversationally, each person talks to God as simply and naturally as to her best friend.

Conversational prayer is characterized by short prayers spoken in plain, everyday English. It moves subject-by-subject; that is, someone introduces a topic, and then others join in by praying sentence prayers on the same topic. When a moment of silence indicates the group is ready to move on, another subject is introduced.

A conventional prayer group often spends time exchanging prayer requests; a conversational group usually bypasses this step and uses every available moment to talk directly to God. Group members hear the requests at the same time He does.

For a more detailed explanation of conversational prayer, read *Prayer, Conversing with God* by Rosalind Rinker or *What Happens When Women Pray* by Evelyn Christenson.

Discussion (45-50 minutes)

The lesson for the next class is reviewed and discussed. One person leads the group through the lesson using the principles outlined in chapter 5. (These principles are reproduced briefly at the close of this book on a page which can be cut out and carried with you for easy reference. Paste it in an appropriate book or your Bible, or slip it in with your study materials.)

Working through the questions in the leaders' meeting gives each group leader confidence in guiding the conversation in the coming class. She has greater familiarity with the material and an idea of the variety of answers that may come out in her group.

Discussing the questions is also valuable to the trainee who has not yet been assigned her own discussion circle. She can serve as an assistant to her present leader. She can help to keep the conversation on track. Because she has reviewed her lesson in the leaders' meeting, she has a ready answer to every question and can speak up when no one else does. Above all, she is prepared to volunteer on the questions of a personal nature. In an emergency, she can substitute in leading the group.

Evaluation (5 minutes)

Because a leader cannot see herself and is often not aware of her own words and mannerisms, the group evaluates the techniques and skills she displays in leading the practice discussion. (What did she do especially well? In what areas does she need more practice?) Using the instructions in chapter 5 as a checklist, group members offer encouragement and suggestions.

This evaluation is extremely valuable in helping leaders polish their skills. The entire group picks up pointers each time an evaluation takes place. It is an important part of the ongoing training program.

Special Emphasis (15-20 minutes)

This segment is used to meet current needs for the leaders. If the teacher thinks the group needs review of some aspect of fielding a discussion, the special emphasis slot is used for that purpose.

This time slot can be filled also with a discussion of how the Bible class can effectively reach non-Christians in the community or how to be better servant-leaders.

Special emphasis can include review of a chapter of a book on leadership. *Be the Leader You Were Meant to Be,* by Leroy Eims, is excellent for this purpose.

Alternatively, the teacher sometimes uses this period to give instructions on how to prepare a short (5-10-minute) wrap-up. Periodically one leader delivers a practice wrap-up to give her experience in speaking before an audience. This prepares leaders to step into teaching positions that become available.

Begin Right

Establish a workable pattern for the leaders' meeting while your class is small and growth will not be difficult to handle. Consistently add new leaders to the group, and never consider their training completed. It must be ongoing in order to shape new leaders for service and to sharpen the skills of those already serving. Do not feel you are wasting your time if you frequently repeat the same training. It will be a review for established leaders and fresh material for the new ones.

Rewards

As the class grows and new leaders are added to your group, you will find that a strong fellowship develops. Working and praying together draws leaders into a close-knit, supportive network. Many leaders say, "This is the best thing that ever happened to me!" or "The women in my leaders' group are my closest friends."

Also, excitement grows as numbers increase. Being the leader of a small class is wonderful, but reaching out to ever widening circles of women gives a greater feeling of participating in God's work in the world. Seeing Him touch many lives gives an expanded vision of what He can do through yielded leaders.

10
Touching the World

"I came here and expressed all my prejudices against the Bible, and you never once told me how dumb I was. Because of your understanding I became a Christian. How could I do anything else after the love and acceptance you gave me?"

"Studying the Bible has taught me to witness. I was always afraid to talk about my relationship with Christ; now I do it automatically."

"I was on the brink of divorce when I began attending the class. Lately, my husband has been telling me he thinks I'm wonderful!"

"Yesterday I did something that surprised me. The checker in the grocery store gave me too much change, and I explained her error to her. In the past I would have marched out of the store glad to be a few dollars ahead. I guess Bible study is teaching me a new kind of honesty."

Everyone who works with Bible discussion groups expects to hear such comments. One of the great rewards of being a leader comes from seeing the changes that occur in women as they study God's Word and apply it to themselves. Non-

Christians come to know their Creator by studying His Word and appropriating His offer of eternal life. Christians mature as they learn biblical principles and adopt the teachings of Scripture as their lifestyle.

Here, with their permission, are the stories of just a few women who attend Bible discussion groups.

Martha

Martha joined the class after years of depression. When asked to define her problems, she pointed first to her relationship with her husband. They communicated with shouting, followed by long periods of silence. Also, Martha had lost her friends. Her negative attitudes and inability to think of anyone except herself had alienated nearly everyone.

A neighbor invited Martha to the Bible class. From the first day she liked the women in her discussion group. Soon she responded to an invitation to receive Christ as Savior, as the message of salvation was made clear in the wrap-up.

People who knew Martha before she became a Christian can scarcely believe the difference in her. Her marriage is much improved. She still battles depression occasionally, but it is not as deep or prolonged at it once was. She trusts God to continue changing this part of her life.

Tricia

Tricia is typical of many. Her story, as told to her group leader, went something like this: "I'd bought the whole bill of goods that a modern, enlightened woman should have a career. At age 34 I got myself off to nurses training, my head filled with visions of career, money, respect from the community, and admiration from my family. Was I wrong!

"Nursing school was tough, but the job was impossible! As a new graduate, I was assigned to work nights and weekends. That would have been fine if my goal had been to get away from my family, but I loved my family! I rarely got to see my husband and kids. Besides, the laundry was never caught up and the house was always a mess! The paycheck? When I totalled the cost of uniforms, car expenses, and the meals my family ate out because it was easier than cooking, I averaged about $25 a week."

What did Tricia gain from the Bible class? Primarily a sense of her own worth as a wife and mother. After study and prayer, she decided that God's top priority for her is to champion her husband and nurture her children. A career can wait a few years. In the meantime, Tricia's organizational ability and love for people will be tremendous assets as she ministers alongside her husband in the high school group at their church.

Factors for Change

What brings about the changes seen in class members? Sometimes it is exposure to a Bible the women have never before opened. To them it's astonishing that there are scriptural principles for building relationships, handling money, and setting goals.

Even the participant who has a biblical background may not have given God's Word a real try. She may have learned scriptural principles but failed to bring her lifestyle into line with them. Head knowledge is a far cry from obedience. The knowledgeable woman often finds her life changed when she begins to obey the precepts she already knows.

Interacting in a discussion group is life-changing, too. This group is often the first encounter someone has with an unconditional type of love. A person who is loved and accepted gradually begins to feel responsible to the group. Once she expresses need for personal change, others will support her in making the change.

Leaders Are Changed

Change is expected in the lives of the women who attend the class desiring to be taught God's Word, but those who do the teaching also change. Every committed Christian is in the process of growing spiritually, and becoming a leader often accelerates that growth. Leaders must study the Bible diligently, pray consistently, and develop the attitudes needed by God's choice servants. Consequently, they find themselves drawing closer to God and stepping out in faith to do things they never believed they could do.

Sally

Sally, a lovely, talented young lady who became a teacher after several years in a discussion group Bible class, described her change and progress this way:

"This Bible class brought me to the Lord and has been my chief source of spiritual food since. Your discipling and belief that God could use me gave me the confidence to step out for Him. As a result I have experienced great joy and fulfillment. It is such a privilege to play a tiny part in declaring God's truth to our world!"

Janice

Janice is a prime example of those who have been prepared for future ministries through leadership training. She had married a seminary student headed for the mission field in Africa. As his wife, she would be expected to teach the Bible to women. Although very shy, experience in the class enabled her to become more outgoing. Her deep love for women surfaced in relationships with women in her discussion group. Through weekly leaders' training, she learned how to prepare and deliver a wrap-up.

Janice testified: "God has never used anything in my life as much as this study. I have learned a greater trust in God, and therefore a greater feeling of self-worth. I learned that all He wants is a willing vessel, even though it is very weak, such as myself."

Janice's husband wrote to the leaders' group of the class:

"Call this an open letter from an appreciative husband.

"I can't begin to describe how thankful I am to God for you women in the leadership of women's discussion groups. It is largely due to the influence of you dear sisters in Christ that my wife, Janice, has been transformed from an insecure Christian into a maturing woman of God who understands that God desires to and *will* use her in the ministry. Through your abundant love and acceptance and encouragement of her, Janice is well on the way to becoming greatly used for His glory."

Janice's husband pinpointed one key reason class leaders grow and mature. A leaders' group is a team that works for the success of all the team members. What one lacks in knowledge or confidence, others build into her.

Leaders grow, too, because they are given an opportunity to develop hitherto unexplored or undeveloped gifts. Many group leaders and teachers say, "I didn't know I could do that until another leader told me she saw my potential."

A woman seldom starts out feeling qualified to lead. As a result, she depends on God as never before and grows to fill the role.

Your Part

You can provide the framework for women to become Christians, mature in Christ, resolve problems and find answers to life's vital questions as they study the Bible. Let God use you to begin a Bible discussion class. Yield yourself to His direction, and begin to see His miracles.

As you read this book you may have thought, *It's exciting what Bible discussion groups have accomplished.* But the real message of the book is "You can do it!" Why not start now?

Section 2

A Study in Colossians

Introduction

The Bible, although sixty-six separate books, contains relatively few themes, each of which is emphasized again and again. Among these themes are love, forgiveness, faith, the Spirit-filled life, witnessing, prayer, obedience, sin, and redemption. Each of these themes (and others) can be developed in a study of the book of Colossians. For instance, a seven-week series might include these subjects:

LESSON 1—Colossians 1:1-14

    Greeting to the brethren (vv. 1, 2)

    Faith, love, hope (vv. 4, 5)
        faith in Christ
        love for other Christians
        hope of heaven

    Paul's prayer for God's people (vv. 9-12)
        to know God's will
        to live to please God
        to be fruitful in good works
        to be strong to endure, patient
        to be joyful, thankful

LESSON 2—Colossians 1:15-27

    The Person of Christ
        Christ, the likeness of God (vv. 15, 19)

Christ in creation (vv. 16, 17)
Christ in the Church (v. 18)
Christ in redemption (vv. 20-23)
Christ in the believer (vv. 25-27)

LESSON 3—Colossians 1:28—2:7

Paul's ministry (1:28—2:1)
preaching the gospel
teaching to develop mature Christians

Paul's goals (2:2-7)
that Christians be encouraged
that Christians be knit in love
that Christ's followers be
rooted in Him
built up in Him
walking in Him

LESSON 4—Colossians 2:8-23

Complete in Christ (vv. 8-15)
circumcised by Christ
buried with Christ in baptism
raised with Christ in new life

Free in Christ (vv. 16-23)
free from rules and laws imposed by others

free from self-imposed religious regulations

LESSON 5—Colossians 3:1-17

Christ-centered thought patterns (vv. 1-4)
seek those things which are above
center thoughts on Christ
expect a future with Christ

Christ-centered action patterns (vv. 5-17)
put off the old
(*don't* be mastered by sexual sin, greed, anger, etc.)

>   put on the new
>   (*do* practice love, gentleness, forgiveness, etc.)

LESSON 6—Colossians 3:18—4:1
>   Christ-centered relationships
>   wives submit
>   husbands love
>   children obey
>   parents are not harsh
>   slaves are responsible
>   masters are fair

LESSON 7—Colossians 4:2-18
>   Prayer (vv. 2-4)
>   for self and others
>   watchful, consistent
>   accompanied with thanksgiving
>
>   Evangelism (vv. 5, 6)
>   witnessing by lifestyle
>   witnessing by speech
>
>   Epilogue (vv. 7-18)

A lesson can be based on a few verses or an entire chapter. Either way, you will never come to an end of relevant, challenging material for a Bible class. You can spend a lifetime studying and teaching God's Word and each week discover new truth!

To show you a sample of the type of material actually used in Bible discussion groups, three lessons from the book of Colossians follow. They are included because leaders planning to write material for classes say, "Give us examples! We want sets of questions and completed wrap-ups to use as models." Three lessons do not present an exhaustive study of Colossians, but they do give a good overview. You may use the discussion questions to train leaders or to begin a "trial class." The wrap-up's will serve to illustrate how one theme can be developed each week.

As my main theme from Colossians 1, I chose how to become a Christian. Lesson 2 contains instruction on how to "walk" in Christ—the followup to becoming a Christian. Lesson 3 centers on how Christians are to relate to the people around them. The three lessons together give a brief introduction to the theology and the practicality of living the Christian life.

I do not have Bible school or seminary training, so my question and wrap-ups do not have the same emphasis a Greek or Hebrew student would give them. I am strictly a lay person, as you may be, too. I often call my pastor and say, "Explain this to me." I refer to books such as Dr. Haddon Robinson's *Biblical Preaching, the Development and Delivery of Expository Messages.* And I pray! My lesson preparation is done as much on my knees as at my typewriter!

The Bible study lessons *you* prepare will probably not resemble mine. Your experience and background are different, and your audience is certainly different. Your material will be designed to meet the needs of the women in *your* class. However, your *goal* will be the same as mine: to lead class members to Christ, help them mature, and enable them to do the same for someone else.

Lesson 1:
Discussion Questions

1. Describe the city of Colossae using information you find in an encyclopedia or Bible dictionary.

Read Colossians 1:1-29

2. In Paul's greeting to the Colossians (vv. 1, 2), how does he describe himself? How does he describe them?
3. Paul had not visited the church in Colossae, yet he thanked God for this group of believers. What had he heard about them? (vv. 3-8)

Colossians 1:9-12 records Paul's prayer for the Colossians.

4. A. Verse 9 notes his petition that they be filled with the knowledge of God's will. How is this knowledge obtained? (Can someone today have knowledge of God's will?)

   B. Knowledge is not meant to be an end in itself. According to verse 10, knowledge should lead to . . . .

5. The lives of the Christians at Colossae were not easy. Paul prays that they will be strong and able to endure.
   A. What problems were these people facing? (If you have access to background material, do some research on this question.)
   B. Why do you think God allows Christians to experience hardship and suffering?
   C. Paul speaks of thanksgiving and joyfulness in connection with suffering. Is it possible to be thankful in the midst of problems? Can you give an example from your own experience?
6. A. "Who is Christ?" This question was asked when Colossians was written, and it is asked today. Who does Paul say Christ is? (vv. 15-19)
   B. Who do *you* say Christ is?
7. A. Because Christ died for the sin of the world, anyone who so desires can be rescued from the power of darkness and transferred into His kingdom (1:13, 14). In your own words, explain what happens when this transfer takes place. See Colossians 1:21, 22 and 2:13, 14, John 3:3-7, 16-18; 5:24.
   B. Has this happened to you? If it has, please give a few details (when, where, how) to your discussion group.
   C. If you are a Christian, write a brief prayer thanking Christ for making you part of His Kingdom. If you are not a believer, write down your present thoughts and feelings about Christ, then ask Him to give you more understanding of Himself as you

study the book of Colossians. (Your prayer need not be read in your discussion group unless you would like it to be.)

8. Paul calls Christ "the Head of the body, the church" (v. 18).
   A. How would you explain "the church" to someone who has never studied the Bible?
   B. Describe the relationship between "the Head" and "the body" (Christ and the church). See Ephesians 1:22, 23 and Colossians 2:19.
9. A. What is the mystery referred to in Colossians 1:26, 27?
   B. Why do you think Paul called this a mystery?
10. "Christ in you, the hope of glory" is a key concept in the book of Colossians. What difference does Christ in *you* make in your daily living? (Or, if you are not yet a Christian, what difference do you think it *might* make?)

Wrap-Up (Family Ties)

Theme: Where we place our faith determines our spiritual heredity and our eternal destiny (Col. 1:13-20).

I have always been fascinated by the subject of heredity, especially since I have a son who is very much a product of his heredity. He inherited most of his father's good points and an abundance of my bad ones. Like his dad, he's easy-going and fun to live with. He has his father's looks and his ability to learn quickly. From me he inherited his allergies, which make him miserable, and a metabolism that absolutely refuses to function in the morning.

My son who dislikes mornings surprised me by taking a job with the postal service that sometimes requires him to report in by 4:30 a.m. In my mind I can picture him straggling in late some day, saying to his boss, "I hope you can understand this: the reason I'm late is heredity." Not "the alarm didn't go off" or "the car broke down," but heredity!

In many ways we are all products of our heredity. None of us doubt that we inherit certain physical characteristics from our biological parents. What we're not always as aware of is that we also have a spiritual parent from whom we inherit. This parent shapes our thinking processes and perspective on life. And it's this parent who holds the key to our eternal destiny. From Colossians we learn that there are only two kinds of people on this earth—Christians and non-Christians—and that each belongs to a spiritual *kingdom* and so has a spiritual parent and a spiritual heredity.

In other words, we all live in two worlds simultaneously. There's the physical world we are born into through our mothers and fathers. Then there's the spiritual world—the realm of the unseen—the world Paul describes as divided between the kingdom of Christ and the kingdom of darkness.

In the physical realm our heredity is determined by the set of genes we receive from our parents. We have nothing to say about it! By contrast, in the spiritual realm we *do* choose our heredity. The choice is made by where we place our faith. A Christian's faith is focused on Christ, a non-Christian's elsewhere.

Dictionaries define faith as belief, trust, or complete confidence. I think of faith as belief plus *reliance*. For instance, I believe my husband will come home from the office every night. I show my reliance by cooking supper.

I live in a city known for the sport of hot-air ballooning. Almost every day in good weather, beautiful balloons float over my house carrying passengers in dangling baskets. Those passengers have faith in their balloons, and they demonstrate their reliance by climbing into the basket. That's faith in action!

Faith is part of our everyday lives. Where we place our faith in the natural, physical world determines our participation in any of dozens of everyday activities. Where we place our faith in the spiritual realm decides our relationship with God, our spiritual heredity, and our eternal inheritance.

The only way to enter God's eternal kingdom is by faith in Christ. Paul tells us that Christ is worthy of our faith.

> And He [Christ] is the image of the invisible God, the first-born of all creation. For by Him all things were created, both in the heavens and on earth, visible and invisible, whether thrones or dominions or rulers or authorities—all things have been created by Him and for Him. And He is before all things, and in Him all things hold together. He is also the head of the body, the church; and He is the beginning, the first-born from the dead; so that He Himself might come to have first place in everything. For it was the Father's good pleasure for all the fulness to dwell in Him, and through Him to reconcile all things to Himself, having made peace through the blood of His cross; through him, I say, whether things on earth or things in heaven (Col. 1:15-20).

The invisible God became visible in Jesus Christ for the purpose of reconciling man to God. A reconciler was necessary because every person who has ever lived has sinned, and sin prevents us from having the relationship with our Creator that we were designed to have.

What is sin? It's our inability and unwillingness to live up to God's standards. It's an inherent tendency to go our own way without consideration for God.

Reconciliation is a healing of the breach between God and man. Christ stepped out of eternity into time and took upon Himself our humanity in order to restore us to friendship with God. As man, Christ could identify with us; as Son of God, He could die for our sin and thus bridge the gap between our sinfulness and His Father's holiness.

You may think, *But that's so severe! The Father could have chosen an easier way than the death of His Son!* But Christ's death points up the seriousness of sin. Romans 6:23 tells us that the penalty for sin is death. We deserve to die for disobeying God's laws, but Christ loved us so much that He took our place. Because of Him we can escape punishment for sin. We can be reconciled to God simply by accepting Christ as our substitute and Savior.

When we place our faith in Christ and rely on the fact that His death paid for our sin, something supernatural happens. We are "born again." Chapter 3 of the Gospel of John tells us that at the moment we receive Christ as Savior, His Spirit, the Holy Spirit, comes to live in us. Through the Spirit we are born into God's family and are given a new set of genes.

Our original genes give us the physical heredity that causes us to resemble our moms and dads and other relatives. Our new genes shape us spiritually so we can resemble our family in heaven. The Holy Spirit within us is capable of molding our character and developing Christ's attributes in us until our actions and attitudes reflect Him. If we give the Spirit freedom to work, we will be so marked by His presence that where we walk Christ will be seen.

How will He be seen? In our lifestyle. Remember the things Paul thanked God for in the lives of the Colossians? He remarked on their love for others, their good works, and their ability to thank God even in the midst of problems (1:3-12). These things were evidence of Christ's nature within them.

Paul also noted what he termed their "hope of heaven" (1:5), hope in this case meaning a truth that can be counted on. Heaven was as real to them as our hometown is to us. They looked forward to eternity with God the Father, God the Son, and their Christian brothers and sisters from every age and generation, because they belonged to a heavenly kingdom even while living on earth.

> For He delivered us from the domain of darkness, and transferred us to the kingdom of His beloved Son, in whom we have redemption, the forgiveness of sins (Col. 1:13-14).

These words give confidence and security to the Christian—but not everyone is a Christian. Some have not been transferred from the domain of darkness into Christ's kingdom. They, too, live in two worlds, a physical one and a spiritual one. They, too, have a spiritual heredity and an eternal destiny.

Those in the kingdom of darkness have not received Christ as personal Savior. They reject Him because they do not believe they are sinners or because they won't believe that only Christ can remove their sin.

Sin is a word no one likes to apply to himself! It doesn't conjure up warm feelings such as considering oneself beautiful, lovely or pure. So, rather than face their own sinfulness, many individuals try to detour around the cross of Christ. They attempt to reach God by doing good deeds, by serving humanity, or even by being religious. Someone in the kingdom of darkness can be very religious. He can join a church or even become a Bible teacher! But how does God see Him?

Colossians 1:21 states that until a person turns to Christ, he is alienated from God, hostile in mind and engaged in evil deeds. He's alienated because he won't accept God's way of salvation. He's hostile because he loves his own sin more than he wants God's forgiveness. His deeds, which may be good in themselves, do not measure up to God's standard of "good" because they spring from the attitude of "I don't need God. I would rather do it myself." This person's spiritual parent is Satan, and his destiny is eternal separation from God.

It was Satan who first challenged God's authority and for that reason was cast out of heaven. He is the prince of the kingdom of darkness and has spiritual rule over all who do not *choose* to remove themselves from his power.

Colossians chapter 1 lays a foundation for making this choice. It describes two kingdoms and explains how Christ makes a way for us to be transferred from the kingdom of darkness into His kingdom. It is only a step between these two realms. That step is taken when we *believe* Christ died for our sin and we *rely* on Him to be our Savior and Lord.

Which kingdom are you in? Is this the one you would choose for your eternal home? If you have already accepted Christ as Savior, these questions are settled. If not, you can receive Him right now by following along as I pray:

Lord Jesus Christ,

I know I need a Savior. Today I trust *You* to be my Savior. Please forgive my sin and accept me into Your kingdom.

Thank You for making this step so easy for me.

Amen.

Lesson 2:
Discussion Questions

Read Colossians chapter 2.

1. Although Paul had never visited the church at Colossae, he used letters to maintain close contact with the Christian community. By epistle he taught, encouraged, and corrected doctrinal error. Have *you* ever reached out by mail to give someone support, encouragement, or spiritual help? What did your thoughtfulness mean to him/her?

2. A. Explain what you think Paul meant when he wrote the Colossians that he was in a "struggle," or "conflict," on their behalf (2:1).

   B. Toward what end was he striving? (2:2-4)

3. Paul paints a vivid word picture in expressing his desire that the Christian community be "knit together in love" (2:2). If you know how to knit, describe the process (or bring knitting needles and give a demonstration). Give your ideas on how the principle of being knitted in love can be applied to this class.

4. A. According to 2:2, 3, where are wisdom and knowledge to be found?

   B. What does this say to you on a practical, everyday basis? See Proverbs 1:7 and 9:10, James 1:5.

5. Colossians chapter one explains what it means to become part of Christ's kingdom. Chapter two instructs those who know Christ as Savior to "walk in Him" or "live in Him." How is this done? (vv. 6,7)

6. A. Verse 8 uncovers one of the traps Christians can fall into when they do not maintain a close walk with Christ. What sort of philosophy or false teaching was Paul warning against? (If you have access to background material, do some research on this question.)

   B. Name some currently popular philosophies or teachings that have led unwary Christians astray.

   C. Have you ever followed a philosophy or religion that seemed worthwhile and logical, yet was based on man's thinking, not God's? Briefly relate a few details and tell what you learned from this experience.

7. Verses 9-15 emphasize who Christ is and what He has accomplished.

   A. Describe Christ using the information you find in verse 9.

   B. Jot down some of the things a person gains through union with Christ. (Look for the phrases "in Him" and "with Him" in vv. 10-13.)

   C. Define the word "circumcision" as it is used in this passage. See Romans 2:29 and Philippians 3:3.

D. Try to form a clear idea of what it means to be buried with Christ in baptism and raised to new life in Him (v. 12). Explain this in very simple terms. See Romans 6:3-10.

E. If you are a Christian, your sins are forgiven (2:13, 14). How do you *feel* when you think about this?

F. Challenge question for those who like research. Explain verse 15.

8. In this chapter Paul warns against philosophies that deny Christ His rightful place (v. 8). He cautions against mysticism and angel worship. (v. 18). He tells his readers not to try to please God through rules and rituals (vv. 16, 17, 20-23).

A. Paul calls rules, regulations, and the observance of special days "a shadow" (v. 17). How would you interpret this phrase?

B. Legalism was not limited to the first century. You may know Christians who focus more on rules of behavior than on Christ. If Paul were still writing letters, what might he say to these legalistic (rule-oriented) 20th century Christians?

Wrap-Up (Walking in Christ)

Theme: When we walk in Christ, we make progress in the Christian life (Col. 2:6, 7).

One of the most delightful scenes I've ever witnessed was a mare teaching her foal to walk. The little spindly-legged baby just couldn't control his legs. Mother would nudge him with her velvet nose, and he would get up and try again. When he got tired he could lean on mother, because she was never far away, but she couldn't do the walking for him. That he had to do for himself.

I thought of this scene as I read Colossians chapter 2 and saw the apostle Paul teaching his spiritual children to walk. It occurred to me that walking is something every creature has to learn. It never comes automatically. For Christians, it's a matter of learning to walk in the spiritual realm as well as in the physical.

Let's look at what Paul says about walking in verses 6 and 7.

> As you therfore have received Christ Jesus the Lord, so walk in Him, having been firmly rooted and now being built up in Him and established in our faith, just as you were instructed, and overflowing with gratitude.

Paul says in verse 6 that before we can walk in Christ we must receive Him as Savior and Lord. Before there can be a walk, there has to be a birth. A colt cannot walk until he is born. Our children can't walk while they are still in the womb. The same is true spiritually. When we receive Christ as Savior, His Spirit enters our lives and produces a new birth. We are born into God's family, and only then can we begin to "walk."

How do we walk spiritually? By faith. Just as it takes trust and reliance on Christ to be "born," so it takes continued trust and reliance to "walk." Faith is necessary because we cannot always see where we're going or why we're going there. We do not know the future. We don't know what circumstances God wants to lead us into or out of. Sometimes we walk in bright sunshine where it's easy to say, "Praise the Lord; He is so good." Other times we walk in the dark and cry out, "I'm afraid! I don't think I can go any farther." In every instance it is trust in Christ our Savior that takes us the next step, and the next.

Walking is always one step at a time. It's one foot placed in front of the other, and that motion repeated over and over again. Repetition strengthens the muscles. Walking in the physical realm strengthens our leg muscles, and walking spiritually strengthens our faith muscles. Colossians 2:7 says that walking builds us up and establishes our faith. As faith develops, it becomes easier to trust for the next step, because we see how carefully and lovingly we've been guided in past steps.

We walk by faith but we are not alone in our walk. We have within us the Spirit of Christ (the Holy Spirit).

Christ is described in Colossians 2:9 as the fullness of God in bodily form. Verse 10 states, "In Him you have been made complete." The Amplified Bible translates this phrase as, "In Christ you too are filled with the Godhead."

Christ is all of God in bodily form. He is forever both God and man. In heaven today is a God-man representing His people. Our needs are His constant concern (Heb. 7:24, 25).

Equally awe-inspiring is knowing that while Christ is in heaven, His Spirit is here on earth residing in each Christian. Through the Holy Spirit we possess the fullness of God—His attitudes and attributes, His mindset and outlook. What do we need to walk in Christ? We need to yield to His Spirit within us.

The Holy Spirit doesn't enter us and overpower our minds and emotions. He is God, but He submits to *our* will. He waits until we choose to ask Him to guide and control our lives. When we face a situation, we have the choice of walking through it under our own steam or walking in the Spirit.

When a friend makes a critical remark, you can retaliate with a criticism of your own, or you can yield to the Holy Spirit and let Him fill you with His love for that individual. When something falls through that you have counted on as you never counted on anything else, you can be dashed to despair or you can draw on the power of the Holy Spirit to give you peace in spite of disappointment. And so it goes with every circumstance of life.

The more you consciously draw on the Holy Spirit, the easier it will be to "walk in Christ" every moment of every day. The secret is yielding.

I'm grateful to the highway department for placing YIELD signs all over our roadways, because every time I see one I apply it spiritually. I have within me the Spirit of Christ, so I have the power to live a Christ-like life. But only if I yield to Him will His Spirit be in control.

As we walk in Christ, we exercise our faith and we use the power of the Holy Spirit. Our practical, daily instructions on *how* to walk come from Scripture.

The Bible is God's Word, Christ's Word, and the Word of the Holy Spirit. It is divine guidance that is never more than an arm's length away. The Bible is an entire library (sixty-six books) filled with God's wisdom and instruction. For instance, just

Colossians 2 tells us such things as (1) be knit together in love, (2) understand who Christ is so you won't be led astray by false teachers, (3) know what it means to have your sins forgiven, and (4) don't think you can please God by following rules and rituals. And every chapter of the Bible is filled with the kind of guidance that helps us relate to God and our fellow men.

Isn't it marvelous that God didn't create us and then leave us wondering who we are and what we're doing here? He has given us a book that explains us to ourselves and Himself to us, a book that lays out a road map for the route He wants our lives to travel.

I learned the importance of a good road map a few years ago when my husband and I visited England. The maps we were given with the rental car seemed to bear no relationship whatsoever to the road system. And in England you don't find a gas station on every corner so you can ask directions. After several days of floundering, we located a guide book written for tourists that contained excellent maps. All we had to do was follow them.

Today you and I have the only spiritual road map we need. The question is, will we follow it? When we walk in Christ we make progress in the Christian life. The Bible tells us *how* to walk, but it won't do it for us. Just as we must yield to the Holy Spirit to experience His direction and guidance, so we must accept and put into practice the teachings of Scripture.

In summary, let me restate the steps you can take this week to walk in Christ.

1. Practice trusting Christ.

It takes faith to receive Christ as Savior, and faith to follow Him and serve Him daily.

You can choose to trust yourself, your financial assets, your friends, or something else, but to make progress spiritually you must choose to trust Christ every day in every situation.

2. Practice yielding to the Holy Spirit.

The Holy Spirit is God without the limitations of the flesh, a person who lives within each Christian. The Holy Spirit can strengthen you, guide you, and enable you to live a life that pleases Him. Your part is to yield.

Again, yielding is a choice. You can choose to do things your own way or Christ's way. The one who walks in Christ is the one who gives the Holy Spirit freedom to direct thoughts, attitudes, and actions.

3. Practice reading and studying the Bible.

Read the Word, meditate on it, pray over it, and memorize selected passages. Let Scripture fill your mind so it is always a ready resource to draw on. For every situation you face, there is a guiding principle in God's Word.

Practice these things and your life will overflow with gratitude. Look once more at Colossians 2:6, 7 lest we miss the concluding phrase:

> As you therefore have received Christ Jesus the Lord, so walk in Him, having been firmly rooted and now being built up in Him and established in your faith, just as you were instructed, and overflowing with gratitude.

When you walk with Christ you have a song in your heart. Your gratitude overflows as you make step-by-step progress in the Christian life.

Lesson 3:
Discussion Questions

Read Colossians chapters 3 and 4.

1. A. Colossians 3:2 in the *New American Standard Bible* is translated, "Set your mind on the things above, not on the things that are on earth." The Williams translation reads, "Practice occupying your minds with the things above, not with the things on earth." Paraphrase this verse in your own words, relating it to *yourself* and *your* thoughts.

   B. Being honest with yourself, make note of what you spend the most time thinking about. Is this the subject that *should* occupy your thoughts? Why or why not? (Consider Col. 1:1-3 and Phil. 4:8). Note: You will not be *called on* to answer this question in your discussion group. "Volunteers only" is the rule on all personal questions.

2. Paul indicates that how Christians *think* is important. Then he turns his attention to *attitudes* and *actions*. Jot down the negative quali-

ties he tells believers to eliminate from their lives (vv. 5-9).

3. A. What qualities does Paul mention as desirable for Christians? (vv. 12-17)

   B. From the above list, choose one attitude or action you would like to develop to a greater degree. Explain why you chose this particular attribute.

4. Colossians 3:18—4:5 establishes guidelines for interpersonal relationships.

   A. In 3:18, Paul instructs wives to "submit" or to "be subject," to their husbands. Define the word "submission" as it is used in the Bible. See Ephesians 5:21-24.

   B. Discuss with the group your *feelings* about submission. (Are they positive or negative? Why?)

   C. It takes strength and courage for one person to willingly submit to another. Christ demonstrated these qualities when He submitted to His Father (Phil. 2:5-8). How can *you* gain more of His kind of strength and confidence?

5. A. Submission on the part of the wife is basic to God's plan for a beautiful marriage. Equally vital is a man's love for his wife (Col. 3:19). Describe love as it is illustrated in Scripture. See John 3:16 and 15:12, 13, Ephesians 5:25, 1 John 3:16.

   B. In what way does *your* husband show his love for *you?* (Thought question: Do you make it easy or difficult for him to follow God's directive to love you?)

6. In Colossians 3:20, 21 the emphasis shifts from husbands and wives to parents and children. Discuss the factors that bring balance and harmony into this relationship.
7. A. What does Paul say about the master-slave relationship? (3:22—4:1)
   B. State the principles found in this passage that can be carried over into today's society.
8. A. Copy and commit to memory the general instructions on prayer given in Colossians 4:2.
   B. Paul illustrates the importance of Christian relationships as well as the importance of prayer as he asks the Colossians to pray for him. He expects their prayers to open doors of opportunity for the gospel (4:3, 4) Just as Paul depended on others to pray for him, someone depends on your prayers. Who do you pray for on a regular basis? (Or, who would you like to begin praying for?)
   C. What doors do you expect to see open for them as you pray?
9. According to Colossians 4:5, 6, how are Christians to relate to those who are not Christians?

Wrap-Up (Relating in Christ)

Theme: Our relationships with people reflect our relationship with Christ (Col. 3:18—4:1).

One afternoon, several friends and I were sitting around a neighbor's pool talking and laughing and eating wonderful, fattening food. At one point, my friend Sharon inquired, "Do any of you put a little mustard in your potato salad?"

Two of us said yes.

"Why?" asked Sharon.

"Because my mother always did," we answered in unison.

How many things do we do because we were brought up that way? We start off doing something to please our parents, then the habit becomes ingrained. We don't even think about it anymore; we just do it.

Other behavior patterns we establish to please ourselves. Some of these habits are good and we're proud of them. Others are not so good and we shift the blame. We say, "The devil made me do it." "The reason I act this way is that my kids drive me crazy." "My husband is so insensitive," or even, "My hormones aren't in balance this week."

Be it good or bad, there is always a reason and a motive behind our actions. Today let's consider the *best* motive—the one that displays our relationship with Christ. Please open your Bible to Colossians 3:17: "And whatsoever you do in word or deed, do all in the name of the Lord Jesus, giving thanks through Him to God the Father."

Here Paul tells us to do everything in Christ's name and to make Him our motivation. When we do this, three things happen. First, our thoughts center on Christ and His interests (3:1-3). Second, our actions show the impact Christ has on us (3:4-17). And third, our relationships reflect Christ-like attitudes and actions (3:18—4:1).

Paul shows us specifically *how* to reflect Christ in our relationships. The first thing he relates is that wives are to submit to their husbands. Verse 18 of chapter 3 reads, "Wives, be subject to your husbands, as is fitting in the Lord."

The Lord designed a man to need a wife who will respect and support him. God never asks any woman to be a doormat! Nor would most men want one! A supportive wife applies her wisdom to every area of her marriage, including decision-making. But in the final analysis she lovingly, willingly yields to her husband's leadership and judgment.

When she submits, she obeys God and supports her husband in the role God has chosen for him. She also encourages him to be a leader in every walk of life. Her influence doesn't end at home. It follows her mate into his career, his church activities and his civic outlets. The way she handles submission touches *every area* of his life. Her actions have far-ranging effect.

Although submission is so necessary to God's plan for marriage, this attribute is not attractive to everyone. When I talk about wives who yield or submit, someone in my audience usually tells me that submission is a cultural concept that doesn't fit in with our modern, enlightened society. What is in question here is the Bible itself. Is it God's timeless message to His people in all ages and all circumstances? Or is it merely another literary work from the first century? Did the God who created man give him instruction for happy, successful living? Or was that God so shortsighted He couldn't see the needs of people in the twentieth century?

There is a wide gap between those who believe the Bible is God's Word and those who do not. I take my stand on the Bible because I'm convinced it is God's Word. My pattern for living and for teaching comes from Scripture, not from a culture that changes its standards every time is convenient.

The Scriptural standard for a wife is that she submit to her husband. Her example is Christ, who submitted to His Father.

> Have this attitude in yourselves which was also in Christ Jesus, who, although He existed in the form of God, did not regard equality with God a thing to be grasped, but emptied Himself, taking the form of a bond-servant, and being made in the likeness of men. And being found in appearance as a man, He humbled Himself by becoming obedient to the point of death, even death on a cross (Phil. 2:5-8).

Contrary to what we are often told, submission does not connote either weakness or inequality. Christ was equal with His Father; there was never any doubt of that. But He submitted to becoming a man and dying at the hands of men. His submission was from strength, not weakness.

A wife is equal with her husband; God doesn't ask her to submit because she is in any way inferior. And she is to submit from strength, not weakness. She is to *choose* to adopt the role that complements her husband's role. Then together man and wife create a unity and bond not possible when they are in competition for leadership. As Paul makes clear, each partner has privileges and responsibilities. Neither is taken advantage of, neither is less important.

A wife's role is one of submission; a husband's role is to love. "Husbands, love your wives, and do not be embittered against them" (Col. 3:19).

I've never heard anyone object to husbands' being told to love their wives. Have you? As far as I know, there is no "rights movement" or organized resistance to this command of God, yet it has to be a more difficult command to obey than the one directed to the wife.

In the Bible, you see, loving is always equated with *giving*. A husband displays the Christ-like attribute of self-sacrifice. He works to provide for his wife's physical and material needs. He's her lover, her spiritual leader, and her defender. His love translates God's love for her into an everyday reality.

How does your husband show his love for you? I've heard women say, "My husband tells me he loves me by mowing the lawn or washing the car." And these things are important! But as women, we want to hear "I love you" spoken in that special way only he can say it. We want to hear him compliment us in front of his friends. We want his arms around us when we're upset. We want love letters on special occasions. It's this tender, open display of love that fills our emotional reserves and makes us *feel* truly loved!

A submissive wife boosts her husband's confidence as a leader; a loving husband heightens his wife's contentment in her role. She may submit to him in obedience to God, but her feelings of satisfaction and contentment come from knowing she is important to him every moment.

How can you and I as wives foster a climate where love flourishes? How can we best reflect our relationship to Christ and set the stage for a loving relationship with our husbands? Our mates are not here; we can work only with ourselves. I'd like to offer several suggestions *we* can put into practice today.

First of all, love begets love. The more loving you are, the easier it will be for your husband to love you in return. Scripture does not directly *command* a wife to love her husband, although Titus 2:4 indicates she should.

I have a friend who displays a motto in her home reading, "The only language spoken here is the language of love." Try speaking to your husband only and always in the language of love." The results may surprise you!

Also, love your husband by praying for him. Influence his day by asking God to step into his circumstances at every point. On his job he needs supernatural wisdom to make decisions; he needs insight into the people he deals with; he needs courage to keep going when he hits a dead end. You can't be with him during all the ups and downs of his day, But God can. So pray for him.

Then, make your home his refuge. For years I met my husband at the door every night with a recital of the day's problems and a list of broken things that needed fixing. Just imagine how happy it made him to walk through the door! I had to rearrange my priorities and reshape my attitudes to make our home a retreat where my husband can be restored physically and emotionally.

My final suggestions for fostering love at home is to increasingly know and love Christ. When the Bible lays out a pattern for relationships, it doesn't say, "Now grit your teeth and do it." It points us to Christ for the *ability* to do it. He is the power source. It's His Spirit in us that enables us to live as the Bible instructs. *In Christ*, wives are to submit and husbands are to love, children are to obey and parents are not to be harsh, an employee is to give his boss an honest day's work and the boss is to be considerate of the worker. When each party reflects Christ-like attitudes and actions, the result is harmony and balance.

But sometimes only one party in the relationship is rightly related to Christ. Is that person released from following biblical guidelines? There is no escape clause written into Colossians 3, but there is a very interesting reward clause.

> Whatever you do, do your work heartily, as for the Lord rather than for men; knowing that from the Lord you will receive the reward of the inheritance. It is the Lord Christ whom you serve (3:23, 24).

These verses are in the context of the master/slave (or boss/employee) relationship, but the principle carries over into every relationship. As Christians, the way we treat others is not dependent on how they treat us. What we do is for Christ. He is the One we serve, and He is the One who will reward us for our actions.

A wife who submits to a husband who does not love her sacrificially submits because it pleases Christ. An employee who takes unfair treatment without becoming bitter will one day be rewarded by Christ. Christ takes note when we graciously set aside our own rights and act toward others as He would act if today He stepped into their homes or businesses. In our relationships we represent Him. He is our model, our motivation, our power source, and our rewarder. Therefore, as Colossians 3:17 says, "Whatever you do in word or deed, do all in the name of the Lord Jesus, giving thanks through Him to God the Father."

Conclusion— Pray, Plan, Persevere

For you to have read this book shows more than a passing interest in a Bible class. Your interest may be in starting a Bible discussion group. Perhaps you wish to incorporate new ideas into an existing class. Whatever your reason, don't set this book aside. Keep it handy for easy reference. Frequently review the steps in lesson preparation, teaching, and training leaders. Then take some action (however small) in the direction you want to move.

A new Bible class, or a new format for an existing one, begins with a vision—a mental picture of what can be accomplished under God's guidance. The vision is shaped and honed by prayer as you place it in God's hands for His direction.

A vision refined by prayer calls for a plan of action. Basic steps of preparation can be taken one at a time. Your daily Bible study hour or "quiet time" can be used to write lesson material. Friends can be consulted about the possibility of meeting with you in a discussion group meeting. Prayer partners can be solicited. A potential meeting place can be explored (a home, a church, a conference room at the office, *any* spot available and convenient.)

Once your plans are underway, persevere. Realize that you will hit times of discouragement when the whole project looks impossible. You will make mistakes! (It's inevitable.) You'll lose supporters along the way, helpers who start out with you and then because of changed circumstances cannot follow through. You may at first have difficulty recruiting class members if your acquaintances are not used to individual Bible study and would rather be "spoon fed." But don't be sidetracked by a few disappointments. If you have a vision and a plan of action, keep moving. God does His best work when things look impossible. Expect Him to do miracles! Focus ahead to the time when your class members will bring other individuals into contact with Him, when those others will experience changed lives because you have persevered.

For Further Information

If you have a specific question not covered in this book and would like more information, write to me at the address below. Your question may have arisen before. Experienced leaders will enjoy passing on to you the knowledge they have gained from practice. Address your letter to:

>Kathy Hyde
>Editorial Department
>Here's Life Publishers
>P.O. Box 1576
>San Bernardino, Ca. 92402

The final words for this book come from a member of a Bible discussion group who has *received* the benefits of the prayer, planning and perseverance of her group leaders. As the book was going into publication, this note was left in the basket used for contributions to pay nursery workers.

IT'S NOT ENOUGH TO SAY

It's not enough to say,
That I enjoy and look forward to this Bible study.

It's not enough to say,
That my world has suddenly become different, exciting, full of assurance and promise, so much less burdened with fear and worry.

It's not enough to say,
That because I am here, Christ has finally become real and alive to me.

It's not enough to say,
That God is no longer a mystery, no longer some awesome, half good/half awful presence, completely out of my reach.

It's not enough to say,
That I have a special feeling for my group leader, for her position is risky business, as she dares to help me in my Christian walk.

It's not enough to say,
That the woman who controls the weekly lecture, thrusts God's words of ancient times, to the center of my heart and *clearly* makes me see that we are talking about now, this moment, this life, this problem . . . not ancient times.

It's not enough to say,
That my fondness for my group grows and grows. It is a relationship unique. We share

the circumstances of why we come together, the situations that have helped us grow in Christ. There is a lot of mutual trust in my group.

It's not enough to say,
with all of you, I'm simply, yet profoundly, "beginning again."

My prayer is that this Bible study can continue and continue. I thank God to be able to participate in it. And I know that MY LORD HEARS ME.

And THIS IS
enough to say.

Gale Powell

NOTE: Page 141 may be cut out and reproduced for distribution to each member of your group.

Page 143 may be cut out and carried with you for quick reference.

Appendix

DISCUSSION GUIDELINES

1. Come to class prepared. You will have more to offer if you have answered your questions thoroughly and have thought through the subjects covered in the lesson.

2. Share your knowledge. Your insights and experiences are different from those of every other class member. Allow them to benefit from what only you can offer.

3. Do not wait to be called on. If you wait, you may forget what you want to say, or you may miss the most appropriate time to say it.

4. Keep your comments related to the conversation. Time is limited, and it's important to cover the assigned topics.

5. Listen thoughtfully. Try to understand the other person's point of view. Maintain an open mind.

6. Be considerate. Check yourself to see if you are talking more than anyone else. Give others a chance to participate.

7. Do not expect the group leader to correct someone you think has the "wrong" answer. (She will not "correct" you, either, if your opinion is different from others expressed.) The leader's function is to facilitate the discussion, not to draw out one specific answer on each question.

8. Above all, *have fun!* Enjoy the discussion!

PRINCIPLES FOR LEADING A SMALL GROUP

Setting Scene

Arrange chairs in circle. As women arrive, introduce everyone.

Leader's attitudes are as important as actions. Think, *I'm glad I'm here; I'm glad she's here.* Communicate this by words and gestures. Help everyone feel comfortable and accepted.

Listen, to both self and others. When you speak, do you make yourself clear? Do you understand what others tell you?

Encouraging Interaction

Assume authority from first moment. Exercise control gently, but *firmly*.

Call on enthusiastic person for first answer. A good beginning to discussion hour is important.

On most questions, ask for volunteers. When volunteers begin to dominate, call by name on class members who do not readily speak up.

Never embarrass anyone by calling on her to answer personal "sharing" question. Rule: volunteers only.

Give special encouragement to each person who answers a question.

When unscriptural answer is given, never say, "That's wrong." Do not allow another member to "straighten her out." Tactfully lead conversation into positive channel. Call on someone who you know will have biblically sound answer.

Give each woman equal opportunity to talk.

Make effort to draw out quiet ones in group. Create atmosphere of security and acceptance. Ask reticent person to read Scripture verses or ask her opinion on simple question.

Maintaining Control

Set good example for group by controlling own talking. Do not teach or dominate. To add color and interest, contribute occasionally, but remember, purpose in leading is to be good listener and draw others out.

Consistently cut off "marathon talker." Say, 'This is interesting, but we're running out of time and must go on."

When member raises question pertaining to subject, ask, "Would someone like to answer that?" Do not answer yourself if someone else can.

If question arises not pertinent to discussion, do not try to answer it. Cover written questions first, and if time at end of hour, go back to question raised.

If question or comment reveals personal problem a woman needs help with, and if subject would help others in group, tactfully pursue. Otherwise, talk further with her outside class.

Never speak critically of any individual, church, or denomination. Steer group away from discussing politics or social issues except where directly related to the Bible.